What Others Are

"I suspect that almost every serious reader of the apostle Paul's letter to the Romans pauses over the famous appeal in 12:1 for all Christians 'to present your bodies a living sacrifice, holy and acceptable to God, which is your spiritual worship.' What does that mean? How do we actually do that in daily life? In *Life on the Altar*, Jim Law answers those questions with clear and practical wisdom derived from the Scriptures. Every chapter reflects not only the personal experience of nearly forty years of Life on the Altar, but decades of pastoral insight as well. If you want to know how to present your body as a living sacrifice to God, you'll find a helpful and encouraging guide in these pages."

Donald S. Whitney, Professor of Biblical Spirituality and Associate Dean at The Southern Baptist Theological Seminary, Louisville, KY Author of *Spiritual Disciplines for the Christian Life*, *Praying the Bible*, and *Family Worship*.

"We are in a season of serious crisis in the American church. But with that crisis comes a giant opportunity - to see a new reformation of the church, a re-forming into what Jesus meant His body to be. James Law, in this incredible book gives us all spiritual and practical help on how to do that! At Life Action we have partnered with him many times and have seen the results in his church and beyond. You will too if you will sink your life into the truths of this book."

John Avant, President, Life Action Collective

"In the same way that he practices what he preaches, Jim Law writes what he walks. *Life on the Altar* is accurate biblical instruction and relevant life application on what it looks like to offer up oneself as a living sacrifice to our Lord. Jim Law knows the gospel and its implications for both the individual disciple of Christ and His corporate body. In a cultural climate that is luring Christians to demand our rights instead of denying them, to celebrate our flesh instead of crucifying it, and to crawl off of the altar instead of consecrating ourselves to it, this faithful brother has brought us a timely and prophetic word."

Jim Shaddix, Ph.D., D.Min.
W. A. Criswell Professor of Expository Preaching Senior Fellow,
Center for Preaching and Pastoral Leadership
Southeastern Baptist Theological Seminary, Wake Forest, NC

"Orthodoxy alongside orthopraxy in beautiful harmony. Pastor Jim has been my mentor and friend for over ten years; his teachings and life examples refresh my soul and strengthen my walk with the Lord. This book is a must read."

Timothy Peng, Senior Pastor,
Lansing Chinese Christian Church

"To borrow a well-worn but still useful Puritan concept, Dr. Law is a 'physician of the soul.' His earnest application in this book will be medicinal to God's saints, dispensing hope to them through the tender kindnesses of God as demonstrated in Jesus Christ."

Ray Rhodes, Jr., Dawsonville, GA.
Author of *Susie: The Life and Legacy of Susannah Spurgeon*

"Jim Law presents the essence of the Christian life as a passionate pursuit of living before God, in his presence, and for his purpose. He explores this *Life on the Altar* out of the overflow of three decades of pastoral ministry, and two decades of training indigenous leaders overseas. This combination of a pastoral heart and insight, along with unmistakable missionary zeal, are what make this work special, as he reflects on the Apostle Paul's illuminating words in Romans 12, which give shape to the book. I enthusiastically recommend it!"

Paul A. Sanchez, Ph.D.
Lead Pastor, Starnes Cove Baptist Church, Asheville, NC

"Romans is *the* book in many Christian circles, and with good reason, due to its triumphant exposition of the gospel of salvation by grace alone through the work of Christ alone. However, its practical portion, chapters 12 through 16, is often sadly neglected in our day. Jim Law's book shines a spotlight into this cavern of negligence and unpacks how the once-for-all sacrifice of Christ transforms and stirs Christians into becoming 'living sacrifices' themselves—not on the altar of a sacred temple building, but in the ordinary spaces of life—in their homes, in coffee shops, and on their jobs. Dr. Law's book will challenge readers to count the cost of following the Suffering Servant in forging church relationships, in engaging a hostile culture, in enduring seasons of affliction, and in pursuing missions. But the real beauty of this book is that its author knows of what he speaks—he is a seasoned pastor, a gifted preacher, and an expert in soul care—a man of God who has often put himself in harm's way in distant parts of the earth for the sake of the gospel. The best tour guides are those who not only challenge their readers but encourage them along the way, and Dr. Law does just that. This book is saturated with prayers and encouragement throughout, and it is my own prayer that it will stir the souls of shepherds and sheep alike for God-glorifying ministry."

Jeff Moore, Instructor of New Testament Theology,
Grace Bible Theological Seminary, Conway, AR

"*Life on the Altar* is a blessed exposition and practical application of what it means to yield our lives in the New Testament consecration sacrifice of true and spiritual worship! This volume is boiling over with what the Puritans once called 'light' and 'heat!' Light represents the sound teaching of the undiluted Word of God. Heat portrays the believer's passionate love for the God of the doctrine and for the sheep of His pasture. *Life on the Altar* is an exquisite portrait of what is entailed in God's holy command to place the totality of our lives at the disposal of the Lord Jesus Christ, without qualification and without reservation! This biblically faithful and powerfully practical edition is a crystal-clear exposition and explanation of what it means to be a living, holy and acceptable sacrifice of worship for the glory of the Lamb! I heartily recommend it to every follower of the Lord Jesus Christ!"

—Ed Lacy, Evangelist & Bible Teacher,
Ed Lacy Ministries, Mobile, AL

"In this volume, my friend Jim Law, has plainly and yet profoundly explained, the beauty, complexity and application of Romans 12. What makes his words most powerful are not only his careful exegesis but more importantly his life message which matches the challenge and instruction this work delivers. Your walk talks, your talk talks, but your walk talks louder than your talk talks. Jim Law's walk talks as loudly as his words in *Life on the Altar.*"

—Steve Canfield, Life Action Ministries

Life

on the

Altar

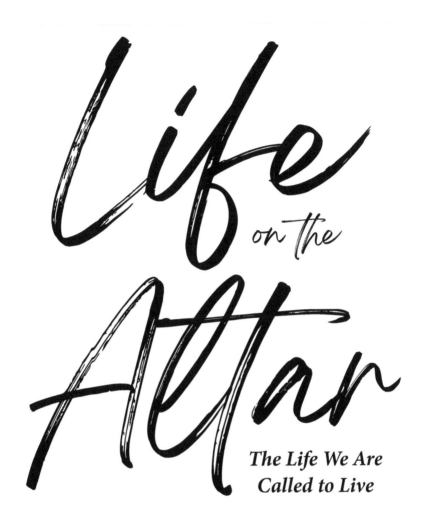

Life
on the
Altar

*The Life We Are
Called to Live*

James B. Law, Jr., Ph.D.

PUBLISHING
MASTERDESIGN
MAKING A DIFFERENCE ONE BOOK AT A TIME
FULTON, KY

ISBN Paperback: 978-1-941512-56-2
ISBN Ebook: 978-1-941512-57-9

Master Design Publishing, an imprint of Master Design Marketing, LLC
789 State Route 94 E
Fulton, KY 42041
MasterDesign.org

Ordering Information: Quantity sales: special discounts are available on quantity purchases by corporations, associations, and others. For details, contact James Law on his website: JamesBLaw.com or www.fbcg.net/lota.

Printed in the United States

10 9 8 7 6 5 4 3 2 1

"To him who loves us and has freed us from our sins by his blood."
Revelation 1:5b

Contents

Foreword

*P*AUL, THE INESTIMABLE CONSUMMATE theologian, plunges the depths of profound truth and scales the highest mountains of God-centered worship in his letter to Christians living and congregating in Rome. Romans is Paul's *magnum opus;* it is the most profound of all his epistles. Martin Luther wrote in the preface to his Romans commentary that it is "impossible to read or meditate on this letter too much or too well." Luther was right. In *Life on the Altar,* we have an opportunity to read much from a key section of Romans (and more) and, as Luther suggested, to read it well.

Romans is the crown-theological jewel of Pauline authorship and theology. From my earliest days of what is now over three decades of pastoral ministry, Romans 12:1–2 arrested my attention, and it has never loosened its grip. Its teaching is liberating. The doctrine that Paul proclaimed—justification by grace alone through faith alone in Christ alone according to Scripture alone to the glory of God—finds its outworking in chapter 12 and onward.

My wife Lori and I met Jim and his wife Gwynne at New Orleans Baptist Theological Seminary almost four decades ago. Jim excelled in his studies, and he ultimately received his Ph.D. Early in our friendship, I was struck by his kindness, zealousness for Christ, studiousness in his research, and faithfulness to the task. I believed that Jim would be a faithful pastor, and that he has been for over thirty years. With sound exegetical principles and theological precision, he handles the text for what it is—the very words of God. Jim's commitment to a high view of God and the full inspiration, authority, and sufficiency of Scripture coupled with his skillful handling of God's Word make him an excellent guide for this book. Jim practices what he preaches; he has ever since I have known him. His marriage and family are exemplary, and his long tenure at his present church is a testimony to his impeccable and loving leadership over a congregation that rightly holds him in high regard.

What we need are not *fewer* excellent works on Paul's masterpiece of Romans, but more. Jim brings a freshness to his joyful task, a freshness inseparable from his kind and compassionate pastor's heart. Jim's pen drips with pastoral concern and pertinent application. To borrow a well-worn but still useful Puritan concept, Dr. Law is a "physician of the soul." His earnest application in this book will be medicinal to God's saints, dispensing hope to them through the tender kindnesses of God as demonstrated in Jesus Christ.

It is with my heartiest and unqualified endorsement that I commend this book to you. My words are not reluctantly withdrawn, and that, in large part, is because Jim lives consistently with the message of this wonderful book. In a day when congruity seems increasingly hidden from view, in *Life on the Altar,* you will find both the message of the book and the author of the book to be of one mind, one heart, and one spirit.

Ray Rhodes, Jr.
Dawsonville, GA
Author of *Susie: The Life and Legacy of Susannah Spurgeon* and *Yours till Heaven: The Untold Love Story of Charles and Susie Spurgeon* from Moody Publishers. Ray is also the author of an upcoming biography of Charles Spurgeon to be published by B&H Academic.

Introduction

*T*HIS BOOK IS ABOUT how the gospel is fleshed out in a believer's life. It is written for the Christian who wants to align, or realign, their life commitments with the purposes of God. It is also written for those who have not yet tasted the goodness of God's grace found in Christ. My prayer is that you would come to Christ with the open arms of faith and join us as we seek to live for Him.

The themes in Romans 12 where believers are called to present themselves to God as living sacrifices drive the conversation in this book (v.1). As we will see, this is not a call to a physical altar in a temple or building. Rather, we are summoned to the altar of God's presence through the finished work of Christ on our behalf. Therefore, the Christian life is lived out by presenting ourselves to Him every moment, of every day, all the days of our lives. This is what I am calling Life on the Altar, and it is the life we are called to live.

A Rich Journey, Not Easy to Describe

Maybe you're thinking, "Another book on the Christian life. Why should I read this?" Well, I don't take lightly the commitment of your time, especially with a book on a subject that is well represented. However, my appeal is to consider the unique message of Romans 12 with the goal of us embracing the simplicity and urgency of presenting ourselves to God for His purposes in this world. We need His power that only comes from being in His presence.

The church, which is often barnacled by many distractions, needs to recover this truth. Pursuing Altar Life is necessary because courage and resolve are essential to stand against the cultural winds howling for compliance. Clarity is necessary when the church seems shackled by uncertainty, confusion, and carnality. We should long for a fresh wind to blow among God's people to clear the spiritual fog and lead us forward to fulfill God's mission to the end. *Life on the Altar* is an urgent reminder that we are not our own. The gospel brings us to such surrender. We have been bought with a price and are called to glorify God with our lives (1 Cor. 6:20).

The aim of the chapters ahead is to help identify adversaries and distractions that keep us off the altar. We need the light of God's Word to guide us and strengthen us for the demands of the Christian life. Solid resolve comes only by returning to the text of Scripture where we find a composite of what it means to follow Jesus.

John Frame has written, "The Christian life is a rich journey, and it is not easy to describe."[1] The believer's union with Christ and the life that flows from it is a rich journey indeed. I also agree with Frame that life in Christ is not easy to describe. A believer is one who has experienced the miracle of the new birth, which is a work of regeneration by the Holy Spirit in unison with the call of the gospel (John 3:3–8; 1:12, 13). This new life in Christ is described as a walk; a race; a battle; and as we will examine in Romans 12, a living sacrifice (1 John 2:6; 1 Cor. 9:24; Heb. 12:1–3; 2 Tim. 4:7; Eph. 6:10–20; 2 Tim. 4:7).

Where Are You Taking Us?

Life on the Altar: The Life We Are Called to Live is divided into four parts following the themes of Romans 12. In Part 1, we focus on Paul's pivot from the most systematic presentation of the gospel found in the New Testament to a gripping picture of how gospel life should be lived out in the believer. Never has a "therefore" like the one in Romans 12:1 carried such a powerful directive.

In Part 2, we examine the emphasis of church Body Life given in Romans 12:3–8. Life on the Altar flows necessarily to life lived in connection with a local church. When we neglect our commitment to a local church, we miss out on the gifts of others and forfeit opportunities for ministry. This section includes the church's call to model Christ's love to one another and highlights

---

1 John Frame, *The Doctrine of the Christian Life* (Philipsburg, New Jersey: P&R Publishing, 2008), 3. I smiled when I read Frame's comment which is the opening line to a 1000-page description of the Christian life!

the ministry of the Holy Spirit as we use the gifts He has given us.

Part 3 follows Romans 12:9–21, a section which includes a series of short commands that mirrors sections of the Sermon on the Mount. Here, we will look at several commands, especially those dealing with our relationships with other believers, as well as with our enemies. These commands are impossible to obey without God empowering us. This is supernatural living in the crucible of various trials. We will focus on living for God's applause in a world with different values, honoring Christ when suffering and pain come into our lives, and living for Christ when enemies and persecution press upon us.

The theme of Part 4—presenting ourselves to God for the advance of the gospel—is a major reason Paul wrote Romans. In this final section, we connect Life on the Altar with the command for every believer to be a witness for Christ. Our hearts must intentionally embrace the call to make known the gospel in every sphere of influence God has placed us. We close with the hope of heaven for the redeemed in Christ. This is a purifying hope that reminds us that "the sufferings of this present time are not worth comparing with the glory that is to be revealed to us" (Rom. 8:18).

A short section called, "Altar Moments," is included at the end of each chapter. My hope is that this will be helpful in making personal applications in individual study or in small groups. I have also included a suggested prayer that coincides with the theme of the chapter.

Three Influences Guide My Journey

I close this introduction with a personal word about three profound influences on my life. The first is my journey of following Christ for nearly forty years, which also includes the major impact of the Bible upon my spiritual growth. I write not as one who has arrived. My sanctification is painfully slow at times, but after nearly four decades of walking with Christ, I can say with John Newton, "I am not what I ought to be … Not what I might be … Not what I wish to be … I am not what I hope to be … Not what I once was … By the grace of God I am what I am."[2]

Life on the Altar began for me in the summer of 1985. I was home from college, and for the first time that I could remember, I sensed my need for God. I would later understand that the heaviness of my heart was due to the burden of my sin. My angst that summer was my inability to resolve the issues of emptiness and guilt with any measure of peace. I remember sitting on a park bench one evening in my hometown in central Florida asking God to speak to me. It was a defining moment, as I acknowledged to God that there had to be more to life than my empty and vain pursuits and asked Him to show me the way forward.

I had received a study Bible as a Christmas gift from my grandparents several years earlier. I had opened the present, seen the Bible, and unenthusiastically, tossed it into my closet. At that time, I thought the Bible was an archaic book for someone

---

2   Tony Reinke. *Newton on the Christian Life: To Live Is Christ* (Wheaton: Crossway, 2015), 268–69, Kindle edition. Reinke pieced this quote together from a message Newton shared in an informal living room gathering. Preserved in the notes of an anonymous listener, these phrases by Newton are a powerful summary of the Christian life.

else. But I would soon discover that its pages held the message I needed most. In this time of spiritual struggle, I retrieved that Bible, dusted it off, and began to read it for the first time. I also began attending church in hopes of receiving some answers. One Wednesday night, I heard a message from Matthew 11:28–30 in which Jesus said, "Come to me, all who labor and are heavy laden, and I will give you rest. Take my yoke upon you, and learn from me, for I am gentle and lowly in heart, and you will find rest for your souls. For my yoke is easy, and my burden is light." Upon hearing those words, I can remember wanting to stand and shout, "That's me! I need that rest Christ promises." Over that summer, old things in my life began to pass away and all things became new (2 Cor. 5:17). I turned from my sin and believed on the Lord Jesus Christ.

A second influence comes from nearly thirty years of pastoral ministry with the same congregation. Shortly after my conversion, I began to serve the Lord through campus ministry and quickly had a strong desire to pursue the pastorate. I discovered in my effort to discern a call to vocational ministry that the only objective criteria given in Scripture for a call to ministry is a desire to do the work (1 Tim. 3:1). For me, that desire became consuming, so seminary was a welcomed experience.

During those seminary years, my wife and I prayed earnestly in our evening walks on the New Orleans seminary campus that God would lead us to a congregation where we could invest our lives for the glory of Christ. That prayer was answered magnanimously in 1993 with a call to First Baptist Church Gonzales, Louisiana (FBCG). I cannot calculate the impact and influence of this pastoral journey, as I have seen God's grace and glory on display through this local body. I will share from these years of experience both joys and sorrows along with the assurance of God's presence. I cannot express adequately my gratitude and love for this body of believers. Truly, I thank my God upon every remembrance of them (Phil. 1:3).

A third influence comes from over twenty years of training pastors in regions of the world under severe persecution. In 2010, I was asked by Phil Walker, president of Advance International,[3] to explore the possibility of bringing accredited seminary training into regions of East Asia. In this area of the world, the church is forced underground because of state-sponsored oppression; persecution is the air they breathe. Yet, the task of taking the gospel into these areas has been one of the most rewarding experiences in my life. Since 2000, I have made over twenty-five trips to that region and have overseen an initiative to bring accredited theological education to pastors who have little to no access to it.

In 2011, we began our first East Asia training center with eleven students. The next year, we were in six cities, and our ministry grew exponentially in the years prior to the COVID-19 pandemic. By the beginning of 2020, we had taught in thirty-six locations with over two thousand pastors and church workers having been enrolled in our program. We have had the joy of seeing nearly one thousand graduates during the last decade. Their stories of living for Christ in the most difficult of circumstances move me to greater surrender.

---

3   Advance International (www.2advance.org) is a non-profit mission mobilizing ministry that offers the accredited pastoral ministry certificate from New Orleans Baptist Theological Seminary.

Forty years with Christ and His Word, thirty years with the same church family, and twenty years on the mission field don't make me an expert, only a fellow sojourner with a deep resolve to not grow weary with living Life on the Altar. In the pages ahead, come and "magnify the Lord with me, and let us exalt his name together" (Psa. 34:3) as we seek to live surrendered to Him.

Part 1

Presenting Ourselves to God as Living Sacrifices

Chapter 1

Life on the Altar

"We have an altar from which those who serve the
tent have no right to eat." Hebrews 13:10

*I*N THE FOURTH CENTURY, Aurelius Augustine (A.D. 354–
430) heard a child singing the words, *tolle lege, tolle lege*—
"take up and read, take up and read." The song was unfamiliar to
Augustine, but he received the message as coming from God and
promptly retrieved a book of the apostle Paul's letters which he
opened randomly in haste. What some might call "a lucky dip,"
Augustine read the passage which first appeared before him. The
text was Romans 13:13–14: "Let us walk properly as in the day-
time, not in orgies and drunkenness, not in sexual immorality
and sensuality, not in quarreling and jealousy. But put on the
Lord Jesus Christ, and make no provision for the flesh, to gratify
its desires."

The application for Augustine was unmistakable, as his life
was described in these verses. By his own admission, he was
a man given over to unbridled lust. It was a word from God

specifically stated in the book of Romans that led to his repentance and conversion to Christ.

Augustine referenced this experience in his classic work, *Confessions*, when he wrote, "Instantly, in truth, at the end of this sentence, as if before a peaceful light streaming into my heart, all the dark shadows of doubt fled away."[1] Augustine was converted to Christ and went on to serve as the Bishop of Hippo (North Africa). For nearly 40 years, he "was known throughout the Christian world as a God-besotted, biblical, articulate, persuasive shepherd of his flock and a defender of the faith against the great doctrinal threats of his day."[2] Augustine was a titan for Christ in the fourth century with an enduring theological influence that would be a significant impetus for the Protestant Reformation.

Eleven hundred years after Augustine, Martin Luther (1483–1546) discovered from his study of Romans that the "righteous shall live by faith" (Rom. 1:17). At that time, ignorance, superstition, and religious bondage were widespread in large part because of a corrupt church system. In God's providence, Luther recovered the gospel which had been eclipsed through neglect of the Scripture by the church. This renewed commitment to the Word of God brought forth the light of the gospel, and the Protestant Reformation was launched.

Two hundred years later, John Wesley (1703–1791) heard the reading of Martin Luther's preface to the book of Romans while

---

1   Douglas L .Anderson, ed. *Christian Classics: Augustine* (Nashville: Broadman Press, 1979), 182.

2   John Piper, *The Legacy of Sovereign Joy: God's Triumphant Grace in the Lives of Augustine, Luther, and Calvin* (Wheaton: Crossway Books, 2000), 42.

attending a chapel meeting on Aldersgate Street in London. Wesley later shared what happened: "About a quarter before nine, while he (Luther) was describing the change which God works in the heart through faith in Christ, I felt my heart strangely warmed. I felt I did trust in Christ, Christ alone for my salvation. And an assurance was given me that he had taken away my sins, even mine, and saved me from the law of sin and death."[3] Wesley had just returned to England from America where he had experienced a frustrating attempt at ministry apart from saving faith in Jesus Christ.

Augustine, Luther, Wesley, and countless others throughout history have come to faith in Christ by hearing the message of Romans. This epistle roars through the centuries as a clarion word on the content and power of the gospel.

Good News for a Broken World

The gospel does not have a shelf life. It's not a message confined to the past. Despite the claims of some, technology and "progress" have not rendered the good news of Christ obsolete. Rather, it remains the power of God for salvation regardless of the generation in which we live. Furthermore, followers of Christ never graduate to another message because the gospel affects every area of life. Whether we are talking about life, death, marriage, parenthood, finances, philosophy, politics, vocation, relationships, or social issues, the gospel is ultimate. Everything else is penultimate. For the believer, the gospel is the lens by which

---

3 John W. Drakeford, ed. *Christian Classics: John Wesley* (Nashville: Broadman Press, 1979), 62.

we view the world. This redemptive message is presented as the exclusive path to forgiveness and reconciliation with the Eternal God. This good news is what the world needs most.

As a boy, I remember a faithful Sunday School teacher sharing with me what is commonly called, "The Roman Road." It was a good seed planted in the soil of my young life. I am thankful for this summary of the gospel. These pillars of truth bring to the forefront our great spiritual need and God's gracious response:

- Our sin has separated us from God: "All have sinned and fall short of the glory of God" (3:23).
- The payment of sin is death, spiritual separation from God: "For the wages of sin is death, but the free gift of God is eternal life in Christ Jesus our Lord" (6:23).
- God has demonstrated His love and accomplished what we could never do, namely achieve reconciliation with God: "God shows his love for us in that while we were still sinners, Christ died for us" (5:8).
- And what should our response be to these truths? We are called to repent of our sins and believe on the Lord Jesus Christ, who was crucified and raised from the dead. From Christ, we receive forgiveness and eternal life through Him alone, for "everyone who calls on the name of the Lord will be saved" (10:13).

Life on the Altar begins here, with a personal encounter with the living Christ. What He has done for others, He can do for you. When you think about what message you will follow or who will guide your life, look to Christ who stands over history as an all-sufficient Savior. I appreciate the words of Dustin Benge who offers this gospel distinctive:

Therapy offers suggestions.

Philosophy offers ideas.

Psychology offers diagnosis.

Counseling offers advice.

Only Jesus Christ, the crucified, risen, and ascended

Savior, can liberate the soul.[4]

The message of the gospel is timeless and priceless, of greater worth "than thousands of gold and silver pieces" (Psa. 119:72).

The Mercies of God

Romans 12 is a major transition in the book of Romans. The apostle Paul writes, "I appeal to you therefore, brothers, by the mercies of God, to present your bodies as a living sacrifice, holy and acceptable to God, which is your spiritual worship" (Rom. 12:1). His appeal to Altar Life is motivated by remembering God's mercies to us in Christ. These mercies are the subject of chapters 1–11 in Romans and are the priceless blessings given in salvation.

So, what exactly are these "mercies of God"? Mercy is defined as "the compassionate disposition to forgive an offender or adversary and to help or spare him in his sorry plight."[5] God's mercy in Christ spares us from our rightful and deserved punishment, namely hell. Mercy is an attribute of God (Exo. 36:6–7), and His mercies are extended to us in His covenant promises. His mercies are said to be new every morning and to never come

---

4   Dustin Benge, Twitter post, January 29, 2021, 5:55 a.m., https://twitter.com/
    DustinBenge/status/1355122472123826177.

5   W. A. Elwell, & B. J. Beitzel, *Baker Encyclopedia of the Bible Vol. 2* (Grand Rapids:
    Baker Book House, 1988), 1440, Logos Bible Software.

to an end (Lam. 3:22 – 23). God's mercy in Christ is on display in Romans in manifold ways:

- God's love and power have been "poured into our hearts through the Holy Spirit who has been given to us" (5:5).
- Power is given to overcome indwelling sin and experience God's sanctifying work, as we are conformed into the image of Christ (6:5–23; 8:29–30).
- God's undeserved favor is extended to those who deserve righteous condemnation and hell (8:1).
- The mercy of the indwelling Holy Spirit is within every believer to guide, empower, illumine, and intercede (8:9, 26).
- God's love is described so powerfully that nothing in the universe could separate the believer from the love of God found in Christ Jesus (8:31–39).
- Add to these mercies: God's patience and kindness (2:4); peace with God (5:1); hope (5:1–5); righteousness (3:22; 6:20); adoption into God's forever family (8:15); heirs with Christ (8:17); power (15:13); and more as He has blessed His elect with every spiritual blessing in the heavenly places in Christ (8:31–35; Eph. 1:3).

These mercies are breathtaking when held against the dark backdrop of our sin. God's mercy in Christ has spared us from our pathetic and well-deserved plight. Could it be that many yawn at the gospel because they do not see themselves in need of God's mercy? Weak preaching fosters this type of response because it is silent about sin and minimizes the tragedy of the human condition (Rom. 1:18–32; 3:1–20). The gospel is also boring for those who, in pride, are driven by a life well-oiled by self-righteousness. Consequently, there is not much tolerance for serious conversations about sin and judgment. The mercies of God are not a stirring topic of conversation for those who think they don't need them, but they are the height of worship for those who cry out, "God, be merciful to me, a sinner" (Luke 18:13)!

The mercies of God experienced in salvation are cherished when we understand that we have not received what we deserve. Paul describes humanity as enemies of God, and yet by God's mercy, "We were reconciled to God by the death of his Son" (Rom. 5:10). He admonishes his readers to consider all that God has done as motivation for giving ourselves in full surrender to God. Based upon these mercies, may we answer the appeal of Paul and, ultimately, the summons of our King to live our lives on the altar before Him.

I Am Not Ashamed of the Gospel

I close this opening chapter with a challenge for us to think deeply about Paul's statement, "For I am not ashamed of the gospel, for it is the power of God for salvation" (Rom. 1:16a). With this declaration, Paul expresses quite a commitment, one we need to embrace in our generation.

The message of Christ crucified was dismissed by many who heard Paul preach. The Gentiles labeled the Christian message as moronic[6] and thought of Christians as atheistic because of their rejection of the multiplicity of gods embraced by Rome. The word on the street was that Christians were troublemakers

---

6   1 Cor. 1:18–25. The Greek word *mōría,* is translated "folly," "foolishness," "moronic."

who disrupted the status quo by separating themselves from the gods. In short, the message of Christ was utter foolishness to them, but to those who believed it, it was the power of God to salvation (Rom. 1:16).

The Gentiles offered one front of resistance to the gospel, and the Jews offered another. With few exceptions, the Jews rejected the gospel but for different reasons than the Gentiles. They considered the message of Christ a stumbling block, because in their minds, it undercut the Law and led to a license to sin. Nevertheless, Paul preached Jesus Christ and Him crucified in every context (1 Cor. 2:1–5).

Paul's resolve in ministry is an illustration of Altar Life and is one of the most inspiring narratives in the New Testament. His missionary journeys in the book of Acts are filled with adventure and triumph, as well as a full array of trials. In Lystra, Paul was stoned and left for dead; however, the next day he revived from his battered condition and re-entered the city to minister (14:19–20)! In Philippi, Paul was beaten with rods (16:22, 23). In Athens, he was mocked for declaring the resurrection of the dead (17:32). In Ephesus, Paul's preaching extolled the name of the Lord Jesus (19:17). As a result, many new believers in Ephesus renounced their occult practices and idolatry. Furthermore, the preaching of Christ in Ephesus brought the silver shrine industry to its knees, and a riot ensued over the loss of profits as many put off their idolatry. Lastly, in Rome, Paul was placed under house arrest. Yet, while he was incarcerated, the gospel continued to spread. Paul's courage and determination in the face of tremendous trial has encouraged believers for two millennia.

There is an important take away from Paul's life for believers in the twenty-first century. The moxie demonstrated by Paul in the most difficult of situations was driven by his Life on the Altar and by his conviction that the gospel was the only hope and power to rescue a humanity spiraling downward to eternal judgment. He had no other message to offer but the one that he received (1 Cor. 15:1–5).

Every believer through the ages shares this common motivation and conviction about the finished work of Christ. We are to join other faithful believers through the centuries and "contend for the faith that was once for all delivered to the saints" (Jude 3). This allegiance of Paul to the gospel is a battle cry of sorts that calls us to choose this day whom we will serve. We need this reminder, because we are often like Peter who warmed himself by the fire in denial of his Savior (John 18:18). Isaac Watts asks a series of questions in his hymn, "Am I A Soldier of the Cross":

> Am I a soldier of the cross,
>   A follower of the Lamb?
> And shall I fear to own His cause,
>   or blush to speak His name?
>
> Must I be carried to the skies
>   on flowery beds of ease?
> While others fought to win the prize,
>   and sailed through bloody seas?
>
> Are there no foes for me to face?
>   Must I not stem the flood?
> Is this vile world a friend to grace,
>   to help me on to God?
>
> Sure I must fight, if I would reign,
>   Increase my courage, Lord;

I'll bear the toil, endure the pain,
supported by Thy Word.[7]

Paul answered questions like the ones posed in the hymn above with his resolve to proclaim the gospel despite opposition. Every believer who lives Life on the Altar is faced with the same challenge. We must remember that Christ is our glory and boast, of whom we should never be ashamed. The gospel of Christ is the only power to redeem our rebel race, and it is the reason we are to live Life on the Altar.

Altar Moments

1. Have you thought of your relationship with God as one in which you present yourself to Him as a living sacrifice? What does this look like in daily living? Is this the image given when the subject of Christianity is discussed?

2. If living Life on the Altar is presenting ourselves to Him every moment of every day and all the days of our lives, how should this affect how we begin each day? How should this impact our attitude? Our decisions? Our commitments?

3. Read Luke 9:23–26 and Luke 14:25–33. How is this teaching of Jesus helpful in understanding the concept of presenting ourselves to God as living sacrifices?

---

7   Isaac Watts, "Am I a Soldier of the Cross," public domain.

4. **Reflecting on the mercies of God mentioned in this chapter, which one is especially meaningful to you? Pause to give thanks for God's mercy in your life.**

Prayer:

> "This is another day, O Lord. I know not what it will bring forth, but make me ready … for whatever it may be. If I am to stand up, help me to stand bravely. If I am to sit still, help me to sit quietly. If I am to lie low, help me to do it patiently. And if I am to do nothing, help me to do it gallantly. Make these words more than words, and give me the Spirit of Jesus. Amen."[8]

---

8   *The Book of Common Prayer: Pocket Edition* (New York: Good Books), 400, Kindle edition.

Chapter 2

The Paradox of the
Christian Life

"Present your bodies as a living sacrifice … "
Romans 12:1

*T*HERE ARE TIMES WHEN the Bible blows our minds.
Sometimes in reading Scripture, we are stretched to consider
claims that seem contradictory but are nevertheless true. This
kind of a statement is known as a "paradox" which comes from
the Greek root, "to appear or to seem." So, at first glance, a statement may appear to be in contradiction, but upon further consideration, there is a resolve that is held in tension.

How we respond to the paradoxes in Scripture will reveal a
lot about our view of biblical authority. Will we dismiss out-of-
hand the Bible as a complicated ancient document with little
relevance to the contemporary world? Or will we embrace it as
being God-breathed and profitable, even those sections that give
our heart and mind trouble? I'm convinced that the Bible is not

only inspired and timeless but is the most neglected resource of our generation.

In this chapter, consider with me the paradox of the Christian life, specifically the one expressed in Romans 12 as a "living sacrifice." If loving God is the greatest commandment as Jesus taught and loving him best means being surrendered to him, then thinking through this paradox would be an important help in that pursuit. Think of how this mindset would bring clarity and confidence to our lives if we approached each day with such a focus.

Pondering Some Paradoxes

Before we look at what it means to be a "living sacrifice," let's consider a few paradoxes presented in Scripture, beginning with the Bible's paradoxical teaching on prayer. We read that God knows the outcome of all things (Isa. 46:10; Psa. 139:16). Furthermore, He knows our needs even before we ask (Matt. 6:32), and yet, we are still commanded to pray (Luke 18:1; Phil. 4:6, 7; 1 Thess. 5:17). This seems contradictory, but prayer is nevertheless the means God has established for fellowship with Him and to receive from His gracious hand.

The doctrine of Scripture is another paradox. Did God write the Bible? Or was it human writers or the Holy Spirit? Yes! Each was involved and flow together to help us form a deeper understanding of the God-breathed text, bringing us to the conclusion that the Bible was penned by human writers inspired by the Holy Spirit (2 Tim. 3:16; Gal. 6:11; 2 Pet. 1:21).

We could also point to the crucifixion of Christ as a paradox. Acts 2:23 records Peter's Pentecostal sermon which references the crucifixion of Jesus, occurring just seven weeks earlier in that very city. Notice how Peter described it to the crowd gathered for this feast: "This Jesus, delivered up according to the definite plan and foreknowledge of God, you crucified and killed by the hands of lawless men. God raised him up, loosing the pangs of death, because it was not possible for him to be held by it" (Acts 2:23). Peter recognized God's sovereignty in Jesus' death yet also man's responsibility in murdering the sinless Son of God.

In listening to Peter's sermon, how would we answer these questions: Who crucified Jesus? Was it God? Pilate? The Roman soldiers? Herod? The Jews who gathered in Jerusalem at that time? Yes! The answer is that all of them were responsible for Jesus' death. This is a helpful example of how a sovereign God accomplishes His purposes in a world of human beings exercising choices.

In the paradox of the crucifixion, Pilate was doing what he wanted to do, namely shirking his responsibility for Jesus' case. Herod was doing what he wanted to do. The Romans were doing what they were trained to do. The Jews were expressing what they wanted done, namely that Jesus would be put to death. And all the while, God accomplished His redemptive plan through the crucifixion and resurrection of His Son.

Understanding how paradoxes are used in the Bible also helps with challenging doctrines like the Trinity. For example, the doctrine of the Trinity is centered on affirming the truths set forth in Scripture about God, namely: God is three persons;

each person is fully God; and there is one God.[1] These attributes are affirmed repeatedly throughout the Bible as God's revelation of Himself. With all paradoxes, the way forward is to affirm the truth expressed in the text of Scripture while holding whatever tensions exist to avoid falling into the proverbial ditch of unorthodox teachings. If we reject these truths, claiming they are contradictory, we do so at our peril.

A Living Sacrifice

When Paul issued the call for believers to present their bodies to God "as a living sacrifice," he used temple language which takes us to the sacrificial offerings under the old covenant. The sacrifices in the ancient world were eventually killed at the altar, never to rise again. Reading the regimen of sacrifices in the books of Leviticus and Numbers can be a tough go. I don't think anyone is ever tempted to want to return to the "good old days" after reading this section of Scripture. Nevertheless, these books are God's Holy Word, and they are written "for our instruction, that through endurance and through the encouragement of the Scriptures we might have hope" (Rom. 15:4).

With each repetition and requirement in the Mosaic Law, I thank God that Christ has fulfilled that old system in substance and with full atonement, which are realities that the Law only symbolized. Paul was not seeking to restart the old sacrificial system, nor was he hinting at a personal payment for one's sins,

---

1 Wayne Grudem, *Systematic Theology: An Introduction to Biblical Doctrine* (Grand Rapids: Inter-Varsity Press, 2004), 231, Logos Bible Software.

which could never be done. The old system became obsolete and can redeem no one (Heb. 8:13).

However, in Romans 12 there remains a New Testament sacrificial system. R.C. Sproul's comments are helpful:

> It is not a sacrifice that we give in order to make an atonement, but a sacrifice that we give because an atonement has been made for us. God does not ask us to bring in our livestock and burn it on the altar; he asks us to give ourselves, to put ourselves alive on the altar. To be a Christian means to live a life of sacrifice, a life of presentation, making a gift of ourselves to God.[2]

Some commentators believe Paul was contrasting the Levitical sacrifices of dead animals with the living sacrifices of the believer's life. However, even the old covenant sacrifices were alive until the moment of the offering. For this reason, it seems best to see the word "living" as a reference to the spiritual life that Christ has brought to the believer in salvation. Thomas Schreiner explains that "the word 'living' denotes the spiritual state of believers. They are now 'alive to God in Christ Jesus' (Rom. 6:11, 13; 8:13). It is precisely those who are alive in Christ who are called to give their lives to him as a sacrifice."[3] To live in this way underscores the paradox of the Christian life as it speaks of both living and dying at the same time.

---

2   R.C. Sproul, *The Gospel of God: An Exposition of Romans* (Great Britain: Christian Focus Publications, 1994), 195, Logos Bible Software.

3   Thomas R. Schreiner, "Romans" in *Baker Exegetical Commentary on the New Testament, Vol. 6* (Grand Rapids: Baker Books, 1998), 644, Logos Bible Software.

James M. Boice referred to this as "life-by-dying," or "dying, we live."[4] Boice continued by stating, "What Paul is saying is that we have already died to sin in the sense that we cannot successfully return to our old lives. Therefore, since that is true, we might as well get on with the task of living for the Lord Jesus Christ. We need to forget about sinning and instead present our bodies as 'living sacrifices' to God."[5]

Paul gives several examples of this dynamic tension. To the Galatians, he expressed in the first person, "I have been crucified with Christ. It is no longer I who live, but Christ who lives in me. And the life I now live in the flesh I live by faith in the Son of God, who loved me and gave himself for me" (Gal. 2:20). According to Paul, the Christian life is a cross-centered life which captures both the living and dying aspects of what it means to follow Jesus.

Likewise in Philippians 2, Paul describes living for Christ as both an effort on our part, and yet all the while, God is at work in us. Paul explains this synergistic relationship with these words: "Work out your own salvation with fear and trembling, for it is God who works in you, both to will and to work for his good pleasure" (Phil. 2:12–13). Again, Paul is not advocating salvation by works but a working out of obedience in our day-to-day walk with Christ. As we present ourselves to God, our comfort and assurance come from knowing that God is working in us to conform us into the image of His Son.

---

4   James Montgomery Boice, *Romans: The New Humanity, Volume 4* (Grand Rapids: Baker Book House Company, 1995), 1492.

5   Ibid, 1494.

The motivation to live such a life is always as an expression of gratitude for God's mercies found in Christ. He has done salvation's work, and all to Him we owe. In his book *Rediscovering Holiness*, J. I. Packer writes, "The secular world never understands Christian motivation."[6] Often, Christianity is perceived as purely a quid-pro-quo relationship with God. In other words, Christians are in it for the blessings, which motivate them to do what they do. To which, we would respond by saying that certainly God's blessings are given to every believer in Jesus, and these blessings bring joy to our lives (John 15:11). We have also discovered that being in Christ, we have been blessed with "every spiritual blessing in the heavenly places" (Eph. 1:3). However, regarding our ultimate motivation, Packer clarifies, "From the plan of salvation I learn that the true driving force in authentic Christian living is, and ever must be, not the hope of gain, but the heart of gratitude."[7] Followers of Jesus Christ are to be a people overflowing with gratitude to God for His abundant grace and mercy upon their lives.

When Christ Calls, He Bids We Come and Die

In the twentieth century, no one brought the paradox of a living sacrifice to the forefront like Dietrich Bonhoeffer. He was a German pastor martyred in a Nazi concentration camp in 1945. His death came by hanging in the gallows a few weeks before Germany's unconditional surrender in World War II. Through his writing, Bonhoeffer warned against "cheap grace" which he

---

6   J.I. Packer, *Rediscovering Holiness: Know the Fullness of Life with God* (Grand Rapid: Baker Books, 2009), 69, Kindle edition.

7   Ibid, 71.

described as "preaching forgiveness without requiring repentance.... grace without discipleship, grace without the cross.... grace without Jesus Christ."[8]

One of Bonhoeffer's most profound statements was made regarding the cost of discipleship. He expressed the matter succinctly, "When Christ calls a man, he bids him come and die."[9] Bonhoeffer's words echoed the strong demands given by Jesus in the Gospels. Those who heard Jesus teach understood that he was referring to a radical call of self-denial, including actual death in the pursuit of following Him as a disciple. The demands of discipleship require daily, moment-by-moment surrender of our goals and aspirations in order to live for Christ.

A perusal of the New Testament, as well as church history, reveals that to follow Christ includes potential rejection, betrayal, mistreatment, severed relationships, and even a martyr's death (2 Cor. 11:23–28; Acts 7:51–60). Jesus defined discipleship as bringing every area of our lives under the umbrella of His Lordship. Far from having our best life now, to follow Jesus Christ is a call to live for Him and to be willing to die for Him: "So then, whether we live or whether we die, we are the Lord's" (Rom. 14:8b).

We are not saved by our performance. And that is a good thing, because we continually want to crawl off this altar of obedience for offers that are less demanding. However, true assurance of salvation is extended to every believer whose hope is in Christ alone, and who, in turn, live surrendered to Him.

---

8   Dietrich Bonhoeffer, *The Cost of Discipleship* (New York: Macmillan Publishing Co., 1979), 47.

9   Ibid, 99.

These Demands Are for Every Believer

I have noticed that when the demands of discipleship are mentioned, many treat the words of Jesus as if they applied only to serious-minded, highly committed Christians but not to the average believer. However, Jesus never divided His followers into such categories. These terms of discipleship are for every believer. When we consider them, they should arrest us because it is a call for the full surrender of our lives. There is no salvation without it.

A great challenge in remaining faithful to the gospel is confronting the widespread deception that one can have all the promises of God and yet demonstrate no desire for Him. Some people view forgiveness, salvation, and heaven as entitlements that are owed to everyone regardless of how one believes or how one behaves. Consequently, this deception dismisses the call to present ourselves as a living sacrifice.

God does not operate according to a human fairness doctrine in which everyone is owed the best God can give. That is not the God of the Bible. I am reminded of A. W. Pink's statement from a century ago, "The 'god' of this twentieth century no more resembles the Supreme Sovereign of Holy Writ than does the dim flickering of a candle the glory of the midday sun."[10] True salvation, and the assurance that comes with it, is offered only to those who come to Christ on His terms.

---

10 A. W. Pink, *The Attributes of God: A Solemn and Blessed Contemplation of Some of the Wondrous and Lovely Perfections of the Divine Character* (Alexandria, Louisiana: Lamplighter Publications, n.d.), 28.

One of the hardest assignments for me as a pastor is being called to a funeral home to meet with a family that I don't know. Usually, they have no connection with a church, which is why I am called in the first place. They are gathered in a room because a loved one has died. Their reunion has been forced by the shared sorrow of the moment, and they want to give their best to have a proper burial for their loved one. For my part, I'm glad that they called; I want to help them in this time of need. However, nothing indicates the spiritual void in this world like these moments.

Some years ago, I met with a family in that situation as they were planning to bury their elderly father. As we met at the funeral home, the family tried to console one another. In an effort to get to know the family, I asked, "What comes to mind when you think of your father?" Slowly in their grief, one of the adult siblings said, "Well, he kept a good garden." Another reflected, "He made a good gumbo." (We live in Louisiana!)

In no way am I belittling the shared joys of a family, especially in a time of grief. But I couldn't help but feel the emptiness of the moment as this family ransacked their collective memory to bring meaning in the face of death. Sadly, there was no mention of God in their recollection. There was no reference to Christ or the hope of the gospel. Our time closed with this exchange. The oldest daughter said, "We are glad that Daddy is in a better place." Her brother offered, "Yes, at least he is not suffering anymore." As I listened to this grieving family, a question formed in my mind, "On the basis of what?"

That is the question, isn't it? So, I ask you what I could not ask that family under those circumstances. On what basis do we receive God's forgiveness and salvation? The urgency of the gospel is seen in that we have a life to live, a death to die, and a judgment to face. And Jesus Christ gives light and hope as we face them all. To present ourselves to God as grateful, living sacrifices is the proper response to the gospel. It removes guesswork on what the priority of life is. This command is for everyone who considers what it means to follow Jesus.

In Lubeck, Germany, there is a stern warning etched in marble outside an 800-year-old Lutheran cathedral. The message communicates powerfully the authority of Christ's Lordship and our call to obey him:

> Thus speaketh Christ our Lord to us,
> You call Me master and obey Me not,
> You call Me light and see Me not,
> You call Me the way and walk Me not,
> You call Me life and live Me not,
> You call Me wise and follow Me not,
> You call Me fair and love Me not,
> You call Me rich and ask Me not,
> You call Me eternal and seek Me not,
> If I condemn thee, blame Me not.

May we not shrink back from the demands of discipleship but rejoice as we persevere by God's grace.

Altar Moments

1. Have you thought about paradoxes in the Bible before reading this chapter? How have you resolved the paradoxes that stretch your mind?

2. The process of sanctification is one in which we cooperate with God. The term "synergistic" was used in this chapter which means "to work together." Read Philippians 2:12–13 and note how Paul describes our effort to live for Christ and God's work in us. Does that challenge you? Does it encourage you? What errors about Christian living does this truth confront?

3. Do you agree with A. W. Pink's quote in this chapter? Is the "god" often mentioned in twenty-first century American culture accurate to the God presented in the Bible? How are they different? Why does that matter? How does this impact your thinking regarding the issues of our day?

4. How do the demands of discipleship presented by Jesus and repeated by the teachings of the apostle Paul challenge you? Why is it important to revisit them in our discussion about the Christian life?

Prayer:

> Gracious Father,
>
> What we know not, teach us.
>
> What we have not, give us.
>
> What we are not, make us.
>
> For Your Son's sake, Amen.
>
> ~Anonymous

Chapter 3

A Living Sacrifice

"But as he who called you is holy, you also be holy
in all your conduct, since it is written, 'You shall
be holy, for I am holy.'" 1 Peter 1:15–16

"Try to discern what is pleasing to the Lord."
Ephesians 5:10

THE ALTAR OF ANCIENT Israel was a bloody scene. Season after season, year after year, sacrifices were presented in obedience to God's command. For a little perspective on the volume of the offerings, we learn from Jewish historian Josephus that at the time of Jesus, nearly a quarter of a million lambs were slaughtered in Jerusalem during the Passover season.[1] This number doesn't even consider the many other prescribed sacrifices of the Mosaic Law that were offered throughout Israel's history. With an approximate gap of 1,400 years between the

---

1   Flavius Josephus & William Whiston, *The Works of Josephus: Complete and Unabridged* (Peabody: Hendrickson, 1987), 749, Logos Bible Software.

writing of Leviticus and the ministry of Jesus, the sacrifices of Israel were incalculable.

These sacrifices are admittedly far removed from our worship under the new covenant in Christ. As a result, we may be tempted to discard them as belonging to someone else. In one sense, that is true. The worship requirements of the old covenant are no longer the pathway to God's presence. However, this does not mean that followers of Christ cannot receive great benefit from studying the Law. The message of Leviticus gives spiritual insight as we consider what it means to present our bodies to God as a living sacrifice.

Let's take a few moments and go back to the altar sacrifices under the Mosaic Law. Some themes emerge as we consider presenting sacrifices as God's people—God's promised presence; God's call for holiness; our need for atonement; and our response of repentance and personal commitment to the Lord.

In the last chapter, we looked at the paradox of a living sacrifice, but why should we present our bodies to God? What does it mean to be a holy sacrifice? And how do we present ourselves to God in this way? How is this acceptable or well-pleasing to Him? I believe answering these questions is vital to understanding the Christian life.

God's Promised Presence

One of the great assurances that God gave to Israel was His presence which offered guidance and bore witness to His covenantal faithfulness. Israel saw the pillar of cloud by day and the pillar of fire by night as a physical reminder of God's promised presence

(Exod. 40:34–38). In the book of Leviticus, God pledged, "I will make my dwelling among you, and my soul shall not abhor you. And I will walk among you and will be your God, and you shall be my people" (Lev. 26:11–12). This was the greatest blessing Israel could experience, namely that God would walk among them.

Likewise, under the new covenant established by the finished work of Christ, we share that same promise of God's presence. Jesus pledged consistently that He would be with those who trust Him. In fact, the last promise Jesus gave to His disciples was that He would be with them always, even to the end of the age (Matt. 28:20). We show our trust in Christ as we worship Him moment by moment laying down our lives and our ways for His ways. As we live in this manner, we live in His presence continually, and God's Spirit bears witness with our spirit that we are His children (Rom. 8:16). God's presence in Christ inspires confidence, courage, and obedience as we face the demands of life.

God's Call for Holiness

The altar of ancient Israel reminds us that God is holy, and He has called us to be like Him. This call to holiness was observed in the Law which disqualified sacrifices that were blemished (Lev. 1:3). No marked or defective animals could be used as sacrifices.

Leviticus 19 is a section commonly referred to as the "Holiness Code" in which we discover how the call to holiness impacted every aspect of Israel's daily life. The chapter begins with God commanding the nation, "You shall be holy, for I the LORD your God am holy" (v. 2). The chapter continues with practical application of the Law: honor your father and mother (v. 3);

keep the Sabbath (v. 3); do not turn to idols (v. 4); care for the poor (v. 10); and you shall not steal (v. 11).

Added to these commands, Leviticus 19 continues with further instruction forbidding oppression, injustice, hatred, dealing falsely, lying to one another, taking vengeance, or bearing a grudge. The Lord concluded with a summary of it all: "You shall love your neighbor as yourself: I am the Lord" (Lev. 19:18). Obeying these commands revealed one's inward holiness that would lead to an obedient life before God and others.

This same command to be holy is stated in the New Testament (1 Pet.1:15–16) and is included in Paul's description of the sacrifice in Romans 12 where he states, "To present your bodies, holy and acceptable to God" (v. 1). Holiness is such a dominant theme in the Bible, and I will say more about it later in this chapter.

Our Need for Atonement

Israel's consistent failure to meet God's holy standards required atonement — reconciliation with God. Every sacrifice offered in the Old Testament by Israel pointed to its fulfillment in Christ who made full atonement on our behalf. We can add nothing to Christ's atoning work. The writer of Hebrews captured the power of Christ's work eloquently: "How much more will the blood of Christ, who through the eternal Spirit offered himself without blemish to God, purify our conscience from dead works to serve the living God" (Heb. 9:14).

Jesus expounded on the root problem and, thus, our need for atonement in Mark 7 when He taught, "There is nothing outside a person that by going into him can defile him, but the things that come out of a person are what defile him" (v. 15). Jesus emphasized that the defiling power of sin came from the heart: "What comes out of a person is what defiles him. For from within, out of the heart of man, come evil thoughts, sexual immorality, theft, murder, adultery, coveting, wickedness, deceit, sensuality, envy, slander, pride, foolishness. All these evil things come from within, and they defile a person" (vv. 20–23). Our sin nature is the root of our problem.

Repentance and Renewed Personal Commitment

One final connection with the ancient altar is the expression of repentance and personal commitment. So, what do we do with our sin nature? We repent and renew our commitment to please God at His altar. The burnt offerings described in Leviticus 1 could be a bull (v. 3–5), a sheep (v. 10), or a bird (v. 14). This offering was given freely by the worshiper, and the various animals were provision for the people based upon their individual economic status. No one was excluded because they were too poor.

The offering was to be without blemish (Lev. 1:3). Under the guidance of the priest, the worshiper would present the animal, place his hand upon it, and then slay it on the altar (vv. 3–5, 11). Great care was given to the arrangement of the pieces on the altar (vv. 6–9, 12, 13), and the offering was consumed by fire as "a pleasing aroma" to the Lord (v. 9). This was God's prescribed way under the Mosaic Law, and again, it provided a picture of atonement through the shedding of blood which would find ful-fillment in Christ.

The bloody altar described in Leviticus is radically different than the one described by Paul in Romans 12, yet the intent is the same. Lessons taught under Moses also apply to believers who offer themselves to God under the new covenant. When Paul wrote "present your bodies as a living sacrifice, holy and acceptable to God" (Rom. 12:1b), these adjectives describe the sacrifice of *our bodies* and that we are to make this sacrifice to please God in pursuit of personal holiness.

Our Bodies Presented to God

The call to the altar in Romans 12 is not to present livestock or birds as in the Old Testament. Instead, Paul emphasizes that *our bodies* are to be presented to God. Stating the obvious, this is because with our bodies, we live our lives. Truth be known, Christ followers today are probably more influenced by Gnostic thought than the New Testament in how we regard our bodies. Gnosticism covers a wide range of thinking but, in simple terms, concludes that the spiritual aspect of life is good, and the physical is bad. Since our bodies are material, Gnosticism asserts that our bodies are hindrances that we should seek to escape. Thus, Romans 12:1 is an important corrective for modern-day believers who may have been unknowingly influenced by Gnostic thinking that permeates our culture.

Earlier in Romans 6, Paul gives instruction on battling sin through the power of the gospel. Notice Paul's emphasis on the body in this chapter. We are not to let sin reign in our bodies (v.

12). In the next verse, Paul advises believers to not present our members (bodies) for sinful purposes (v. 13). Lastly, Paul proclaims that the power of God's grace in Jesus Christ strengthens us to overcome the pull of sin with ultimate victory: "For sin will have no dominion over you, since you are not under law but under grace" (v. 14). What connection is Paul making between one's body and putting off sin? And why is he making this connection?

Paul's emphasis on presenting our bodies includes the totality of who we are, including our spiritual being, the essence of our person. Schreiner's comments are helpful in seeing that the word "bodies" is a reference "to the whole person and stresses that consecration to God involves the whole person ... One cannot consign dedication to God to the spirit and neglect the body. Genuine commitment to God embraces every area of life and includes the body in all of its particularity and concreteness."[2] Nothing is off limits in our surrender to Christ—our heart, our mind, our eyes, our tongue, our hands, our feet, our dreams, our goals, our plans, and our will.

These thoughts remind me of the significance of August 12th in my own spiritual journey, as it is the date I was ordained into gospel ministry. I have a ritual every year on this day. I get down on my knees and thank God for the calling and privilege of proclaiming the unsearchable riches of Christ. For my ordination service in 1991, I was given the opportunity to select music that was especially meaningful to me. The hymn by Frances Havergal

2   Schreiner, *Romans*, 644.

came to my mind. I was introduced to it for the first time in the summer of my conversion. The opening stanza reads:

> Take my life and let it be
>> Consecrated, Lord, to Thee;
> Take my hands and let them move
>> At the impulse of Thy love,
> At the impulse of Thy love.[3]

Havergal continues in the following stanzas with references to "my feet," "my voice," "my silver and my gold," "my moments and my days," "my will," and "my heart." This captures the command given by the apostle Paul and what it means to live Life on the Altar. All parts of a believer are to be offered to Christ in surrender to Him. It is in this position of surrender that we freely and gratefully give to Christ all that we are and hope to be, and in so doing, we please God.

Living to Please God—Is That Even Possible?

The sacrifices of the old covenant were said to be "a soothing aroma to the Lord" (Lev. 1:9). Sacrifices offered in faith and obedience are well-pleasing to God. This is an important truth to internalize.

The Christian life is to be lived for the purpose of pleasing our gracious God. Our motivation for doing so is God's great mercy extended to us. Life on the Altar is a daily walk in which we aim to please Him (2 Cor. 5:9). Our efforts in this life are a continual quest of trying "to discern what is pleasing to the Lord" (Eph. 5:10). This does not grow a dull story; on the contrary, it is a life

---

3   Frances Havergal, "Take My Life, and Let It Be Consecrated," public domain.

of abundant joy that comes from a God who rewards those who seek him (Heb. 11:5–6). By God's grace, we can live lives that are well-pleasing and acceptable to Him. But, how?

At the end of the old covenant era, the prophet Malachi preached against the spiritual slide of God's people. In Malachi's day, it was common practice to offer blemished sacrifices to God. With strong sarcasm, he rebuked the flawed offerings on the altar of worship: "When you offer blind animals in sacrifice, is that not evil? And when you offer those that are lame or sick, is that not evil? Present that to your governor; will he accept you or show you favor? says the LORD of hosts" (Mal. 1:8). The blind and maimed animals given to the Lord were indicators of their wayward hearts. In essence, Malachi was saying, "You give to the Lord what you would never give to your governor, or anyone else for that matter. That's pathetic, and worse, it's evil."

We battle the same heart tendencies as those in Malachi's day. Our offerings are often marred by mediocrity and apathy. Our approach to the altar is to sacrifice at a discount. Rare is the testimony of King David who said, "I will not offer burnt offerings to the LORD my God that cost me nothing" (2 Sam. 24:24). How do we overcome our lethargy? We look to Jesus.

In the Gospels it was said of Jesus that He always did that which pleased His Father (Matt. 3:8). Likewise, as we follow Him, as we seek to live as Christ lived on earth, we model the example of our Savior who "loved us and gave himself up for us, a fragrant offering and sacrifice to God" (Eph. 5:2). When we demonstrate Christ's love in this world, it is a pleasing sacrifice in the courts of heaven.

Some years ago, Paul Harvey shared a true story of a woman and her frozen Thanksgiving turkey. The Butterball Company set up a telephone hotline to answer consumers' questions about preparing holiday turkeys. This woman called to inquire about cooking a turkey that had been in the bottom of her freezer for 23 years. The Butterball representative told her that while the turkey would probably be safe to eat, the flavor would have deteriorated to such a degree that she would not recommend eating it. The caller replied, "That's what I thought. We'll give the turkey to our church."[4]

Because we are prone to offer to God what we would never give to others, or even accept for ourselves, we need repeatedly to be challenged to give our all — our entire being. The application for us is clear. All our being is to be presented to God with a desire to please Him and to pursue holiness.

Holiness as a Life Pursuit

When is the last time you were asked, "How's your pursuit of holiness going?" It's probably been a while. We would expect that to be a regular question among Christians considering the massive treatment the subject of holiness receives in the Bible. With such an emphasis in God's Word, why is holiness often viewed by believers as undesirable, suffocating, and maybe even boring? We don't have to look very deep into the Bible to find that such thinking is out of order. Consider the contrast between the

---

4   Christianity Today, "Giving the Worst to the Church," preachingtoday.com. https://www.preachingtoday.com/illustrations/2007/august/14428.html (accessed July 17, 2021).

prevailing attitude toward holiness in contemporary Christianity, and the way Scripture references this prized pursuit.

In Exodus 15:11, when Israel is celebrating God's deliverance through the parting of the Red Sea, in their worship, they proclaim, "Who is like you, majestic in holiness, awesome in glorious deeds, doing wonders?" Israel extolled the greatness of God and specifically mentioned the majesty of His holiness. Similarly, holiness is described as beautiful in Psalm 29:2: "Worship the LORD in the splendor of holiness."

Psalm 15 pictures the holy hill of the Lord as the place we should long to dwell. For the psalmist, the holy hill referred to Mount Zion, where the temple was located. The psalm begins with a question, "Who shall sojourn in your tent? Who shall dwell on your holy hill?" (v.1). How many among us are even asking this question? Furthermore, throughout the psalm, the writer highlights the integrity and personal holiness of the one who truly worships God.

One of the greatest motivations for pursuing holiness is found in Hebrews 12:14. Here the writer admonishes, "Strive for peace with everyone, *and for the holiness without which no one will see the Lord*" (italics mine). Wow! This verse warns that holiness is a prerequisite for heaven. What type of holiness is required? A *personal* holiness that comes from a surrendered life to Christ. As a believer, if I am not serious about living a life set apart for the glory of God, I have a major spiritual problem and every reason to question my standing with Him. Why would I think I'm going to heaven if I am not bearing any similarity to the God of heaven?

In his book, *Union with Christ,* Rankin Wilbourne diagnoses the problem well when he refers to holiness as "The Big Broccoli in the Sky."[5] Wilbourne explains, "Holiness is like broccoli for many of us. We know we are supposed to want it, but we don't, not really. And we might even think the good news is that we no longer need to pursue it."[6]

Wilbourne challenges the prevailing neglect of holiness among God's people: "God wants us to grow in holiness, not as some sort of test or punishment, not even just as preparation for the future, but because he wants us to enjoy life with him more. The more we grow in holiness, the more we can enjoy his presence. He wants us not simply to press on but to soar."[7] Or as J. I. Packer wrote, "In reality, holiness is the goal of our redemption. As Christ died in order that we may be justified, so we are justified in order that we may be sanctified and made holy."[8] Holiness, originating from a position of surrender to God, describes and motivates a life well-pleasing to Him.

Altar Moments

1. Read Leviticus 1. What impressions come to mind as you read about the altar of Israel? How does this impact your thoughts on Christ's once-for-all sacrifice for sin?

---

5   Rankin Wilbourne, *Union with Christ: The Way to Know and Enjoy God* (Colorado Springs: David C. Cook, 2016), 172.

6   Ibid.

7   Ibid. 186.

8   Packer, *Rediscovering Holiness*, 33.

2. One of the great promises of the Bible is God's presence with His people. Jesus spoke about this in the Upper Room discourse of John's Gospel. What do the following verses say for those who trust in Christ?

> John 14:1–6
> John 14:23

3. Why is holiness often neglected among believers? What adjustments need to be made in our lives to pursue holiness?

4. Read Malachi 1. Do you agree with the statement in this chapter that we often give to God what we would not give to others? Is it possible to present ourselves to God in such a way that it is well-pleasing and acceptable to Him? What is an example of such a life?

Prayer:

Dear Lord Jesus Christ,

Thank You for Your saving work. Through Your sinless life, Your substitutionary death, and Your glorious resurrection, I have passed from death to life. Because of Your rich mercies, I present myself to You this day as a living, holy, and acceptable sacrifice. I know that I could never earn forgiveness, so my motivation for serving You is an ever-growing gratitude. Thank You for the reminder of my need to pursue holiness without which no one will see You. Lord, help me to love what You love and hate what You hate. Keep me from self-righteousness and pride and may the fragrance of my life be well-pleasing in Your sight. Amen.

Chapter 4

Worship That Makes Perfect Sense

"You yourselves like living stones are being built up as a spiritual house, to be a holy priesthood, to offer spiritual sacrifices acceptable to God through Jesus Christ." 1 Peter 2:5

MY FAMILY AND I went to a theme park several years ago. After watching the killer whales perform their tricks, we exited the aqua theatre. As we left the facility, I noticed they had put the word "BELIEVE" on the large screen above. My first thoughts were, "What do they want us to believe? Believe in the power of killer whales? Believe in ourselves? Believe in belief? Believe what?" After kicking these questions around in my mind, it reminded me that the words "faith" and "believe" have been lost in our culture to a hundred conflicting and vague definitions.

When we read the Bible, there is also an announcement to "BELIEVE." However, the Scripture does not leave it open-ended. Jesus began His earthly ministry with this message, "The time is fulfilled, and the kingdom of God is at hand; repent and believe in the gospel" (Mark 1:15). The Christian faith is not a fill-in-the-blank belief system. We are not allowed to custom design the claims of Christ as if we were building a house where we pick and choose the colors, the fixtures, and the flooring. The call to believe in the Bible is not a trip through the buffet line at a restaurant where we pick and choose what we want.

On the contrary, biblical faith, true saving faith, has substance (Heb. 11:1) and is evident through an obedient life to Christ. Jesus said, "Why do you call me 'Lord, Lord,' and not do what I tell you?" (Luke 6:46). The life of faith, indeed Life on the Altar, is one that is given to the obedience of faith (Rom. 1:5; 6:16; 16:26).

As we consider our response to the gospel outlined in Romans 1–11, we are called to believe on the Lord Jesus Christ. This saving faith is demonstrated through obedience to God's commands and surrender in every aspect of our lives. We also discover in Romans 12:1 that such a life is "spiritual worship."

We emphasized in chapter 2 that the Bible often presents doctrine in tension. We also underscored that biblical truth is not irrational or contradictory. True faith, the faith referred to in the Bible, possesses three components that rescue it from a "leap-in-the-dark" understanding.

Our Faith Has Content

Biblical faith is anchored to foundational truths centered on the life, death, and resurrection of Jesus Christ. Christ really came. He really walked on this earth. He really lived a sinless life. He really taught, healed, suffered, bled, and died. He really rose from the dead. He really commissioned His disciples to go global with the good news of what He accomplished. And, we are talking about it now, because they obeyed what He told them to do. Biblical faith has specific content. It is not a wax nose that can be molded and shaped into what we think is best. However, there is more to faith than knowing facts about Jesus.

Our Faith Includes Agreement with the Content

Does the good news of Jesus Christ resonate in your heart as true? Is there within you a resounding "yes" to this message of Jesus? Of all the worldviews you could embrace, do you find the message of Christ superior over them all? True faith requires agreement with the gospel in order to receive the remedy it promises.

Our Faith Is Actual Trust in Jesus as the Son of God and Savior

Agreement with the content of the gospel leads to personal trust in Christ alone. This faith relationship is not a belief in a religious icon, but upon a living Lord who "has all authority in heaven and on earth" (Matt. 28:18). The writer of Hebrews explains that we must believe that God is who He says He is: "For without faith it is impossible to please Him, for he who comes to God must believe that He is" (Heb. 11:6 NKJV). And the Bible was written that we would believe this message (1 John 5:13).

Biblical faith has historical content, requires agreement with that content, and must demonstrate personal trust in Christ.

Living by Faith, Living to Worship

In Romans 12:1, what did Paul mean by "spiritual worship?" How should this inform our understanding of the living sacrifice we have been discussing? How should this help us live for Christ as we approach each day and each moment of our lives?

The term "spiritual worship" requires some work to understand. There are two words used in the Greek text, *logikos* and *latreia*. *Logikos* is the source for the English word "logical," and it can mean either "rational, genuine, true" [1] or in a figurative sense, "spiritual." [2] *Latreia* can be translated worship or service and is used in describing religious service to God. [3] Consequently, the translations vary: The King James Version translates these words as, "your reasonable service," and the English Standard Version as "your spiritual worship." The New Living Translation brings emphasis to the living sacrifice of ourselves to God as "truly the way to worship him." So, whether we translate this phrase as "reasonable service," or "spiritual worship," it seems to capture both ideas: our spiritual worship is logical and reasonable service considering God's mercies extended to us in the gospel.

1   J. P. Louw, and E. A. Nida, (1996), *Greek-English Lexicon of the New Testament: Based on Semantic Domains 2nd edition., Vol. 1* (New York: United Bible Societies, 1996), 674, Logos Bible Software.
2   Ibid.
3   Ibid, 532.

Furthermore, Life on the Altar before God resulting in spiritual worship is all encompassing. John Stott brings an important word of application here: "What ... is this living sacrifice, this rational, spiritual worship? It is not to be offered in the temple courts or in the church building, but rather in home life and in the marketplace. It is the presentation of our bodies to God."[4]

This viewpoint is vital to our understanding of Christian worship which is often relegated to a building or a routine. True spiritual worship involves our mind, our reason, our body, and our intellect offered to God in moment-by-moment obedience in all areas of our lives. Presenting ourselves to God in this way is a reasonable, logical response. By contrast, to live for yourself and the fleeting pleasures of this world is the path of a fool which leads to destruction (Psa. 1:4–6). Christian, your daily worship of God makes perfect sense in light of His abundant grace upon your life. God is worthy of such an offering, and it is the privilege of every believer to present themselves in this way.

This truth of living for the glory of God was recovered by the Reformers who saw from Scripture that all of life was to be lived *Coram Deo*, a Latin phrase meaning "before the face of God." Why are we hesitant to live before God in this way? Why are we prone to give the scraps of our lives to Him who has extended to us His stunning grace in Christ?

Perhaps we think we will be ripped off or miss out on something better. Perhaps we are in doubt of God's promises, so we hedge our losses with blemished, half-hearted offerings. How

---

4   John R. W. Stott, *The Message of Romans: God's Good News for the World* (Downers Grove, IL: InterVarsity Press, 2001), 321, Logos Bible Software.

foolish! For those who walk with God will lack no good thing (Psa. 84:11). Again, I refer to the example of David when he said, "I will not offer burnt offerings to the LORD my God that cost me nothing" (2 Sam. 24:24). David spoke these words after his prideful display in ordering the census of Israel. God's chastening hand came upon the nation because of David's pride. This man, whose transgressions were well documented (2 Sam. 11–12; Psa. 51), nevertheless lived in gratitude for the Lord's mercies and was determined not to offer God the "leftovers" of his life.

The text of Romans 12 and, specifically, the call for spiritual worship, brings us once again to what God wants most. He wants us, *all* of us, and it is His prerogative to ask for it. With his usual precision Boice writes,

> You will begin to understand the Christian life when you understand that God does not want your money or your time without yourself. You are the one for whom Jesus died. You are the one he loves. So, when the Bible speaks of reasonable service, as it does here, it means that you are the one God wants. It is sad if you try to substitute things for that, the greatest gift.[5]

To follow Jesus Christ is a faith relationship in which we give ourselves to Him who has redeemed our lives from destruction and crowned us with lovingkindness and tender mercy (Psa. 103:4). Living by faith leads us to true, logical, and reasonable worship of the One True God, which makes perfect sense!

---

5   Boice, *Romans*, 1517.

Worship Starts with Relationship

Our personal worship is the ballast that keeps us steady in a world of jarring distractions and profound disappointments. As we have seen in Romans 12:1, Life on the Altar is God's call to worship through the continual presentation of ourselves to Him. Worship takes many forms in the Christian life. From acts of obedience, to private, as well as corporate, expressions of devotion to God. Worship keeps us focused on the One who keeps us running the race that ends at His feet.

Some years back, I read David McCullough's biography of John Adams, the second president of the United States. When I came to the end of this exhaustive biography, I felt like I knew John Adams. By saying that, I never thought that I would run into him at the post office. After all, he died two centuries ago. He's dead. The only way I can encounter him is on the pages of his biography.[6]

Bob Kauflin makes a helpful connection here with true worship: "I wonder how many of us, when it comes to knowing and worshiping God, approach him like the main figure of a biography? We learn what he did in the past but don't expect to engage with him. We hear and read his Word, but it's no more than history, principles, commands, rules, and promises in a book. A unique book to be sure, but just a book."[7] Kauflin continued by reminding us that we need to remember that "the Bible isn't

---

6 I got the idea about using a historical figure in this way from Bob Kauflin, *True Worshipers: Seeking What Matters to God* (Wheaton: Crossway, 2015), 127–29. Kauflin used Alexander Hamilton, and I had a similar connection when reading John Adams' biography.

7 Ibid, 128.

the biography of a distant, absent, or dead deity."[8] John Adams is dead; Jesus Christ is alive. "Scripture speaks of a God who is near, a God who is active, a God who breaks into the present—a God with whom we can engage. A God who is personal."[9]

Worship centers on knowing our risen Savior Jesus and is vital to vibrant Christian living. Four prominent themes—we are redeemed to worship, to live in awe of the God who reigns, to behold the beauty of the Lord, and to worship as a way of life—should guide our thinking about this priority of the Christian life.

Redeemed to Worship

In the fullness of time, Christ came and fulfilled what was required for redemption (Gal. 4:4–7). Through His death, reconciliation with God has come to a fallen race. Those who trust in Christ are restored to offer true worship in spirit and truth (John 4:23–24). This is a foretaste of the great worship gathering of all God's redeemed who will worship Him forever and ever in the new creation (Rev. 7:9–12). This message of redemption, this good news in Christ, brings transformation to our hearts of stone, hardened by sin, and gives to us a new heart with longings and desires to worship Him.

We are unable to worship in spirit and truth apart from God's grace in Christ. Sin has dealt a crushing blow to our abilities to think Godward. Our worship is made possible and sustained

---

8   Ibid.
9   Ibid.

through the grace found in Christ. His mercies which are new each morning fuel a faithful life of worship.

Living in Awe of the God Who Reigns

The Bible pictures God as the One who is high and lifted up. He is transcendent and sovereign. He sits in the heavens and does whatever He pleases (Psa. 115:3). The earth is the Lord's and the fullness of it is His doing (Psa. 24:1). Because of these truths, we are to live in awe of Him who reigns.

The prophet Isaiah captures the awesome power of God through his prophecy. Isaiah 40 is a major transition in the prophet's work. After thirty-nine chapters of judgment because of sin, Isaiah 40 begins with these words, "Comfort, comfort my people, says your God. Speak tenderly to Jerusalem, and cry to her that her warfare is ended, that her iniquity is pardoned, that she has received from the LORD's hand double for all her sins" (Isa. 40:1–2).

Paul Tripp in his book, *Awe: Why It Matters for Everything We Think, Say, and Do*, provides this insight on the help of Isaiah 40 to live in awe of our great God:

> The comfort of Isaiah 40 is that it gives us the only worldview that has eternal hope embedded in it. Isaiah 40 comforts us not because it helps us understand life or divine the future but because it reminds us of the glory of the God who rules in majesty over all the things that would otherwise rob us of comfort and hope. We need Isaiah to say to us again and again, "Here is your God!" And we need to let the awesome glory of his description of our

God wash our hearts clean of cynicism, doubt, fear, discouragement, anxiety, worry, and control.[10]

We need ongoing adjustments to our viewpoint like the one Isaiah 40 gives, so our eyes will be lifted to see and worship the God who reigns.

Beholding the Beauty of the Lord

In the Psalms, King David recorded a driving commitment in his life when he declared:

> **One thing have I asked of the LORD, that will I seek after: that I may dwell in the house of the LORD all the days of my life, to gaze upon the beauty of the LORD and to inquire in his temple. (Psa. 27:4)**

From this psalm, we see David's laser-focus on the Lord in personal worship. Clearly, it is the consuming commitment of his heart, as he commits to seek the Lord and dwell in His presence all the days of his life. His longing in worship is "to gaze upon the beauty of the Lord" (v. 4). This is an amazing expression. Worship requires determination motivated by conviction that God is the greatest, most beautiful treasure we could ever have.

David mentions "the beauty of the Lord," yet this is an attribute of God that doesn't get as much attention as others. When we think of God's attributes we think of His sovereignty, omniscience, omnipresence, omnipotence, holiness, and love, but His beauty doesn't often make our short list of attributes. Lutheran

---

10 Paul David Tripp, *Awe: Why It Matters for Everything We Think, Say, and Do* (Wheaton: Crossway, 2015), 140, Kindle edition.

scholar, H. C. Leupold provides the following thought, "The 'kindness' of the Lord, *no'am*, is a term that is difficult to render. It means 'pleasantness,' 'graciousness' and the like.... It means nothing more than to discover anew how gracious and merciful the good Lord really is."[11] For David, God's presence was the place in which he longed to live, because it was pleasant, gracious, good, and in a word, a beautiful place. Such is the testimony of one who seeks to live in God's presence.

Worship as a Way of Life

In a right relationship with God through Christ, we become true worshipers of the God who reigns, beholding His beauty. From this joyful, secure position, worship becomes a way of life for the believer. Everything becomes an opportunity to present to God our obedience and worship. Following the example of David, we learn to live life in the presence of God which leads us to moment-by-moment acknowledging Him. For example, Ray Ortlund offers pastoral guidance on simple ways to pray throughout the day:

> Thank you, Lord.
>
> > Give me strength, Lord.
>
> Help me, Lord.
>
> > You know best, Lord.
>
> Forgive me, Lord.
>
> > I surrender, Lord.

---

11 H. C. Leupold, *Exposition of the Psalms* (Grand Rapids, MI: Baker Book House, 1959), 236, Logos Bible Software.

Keep me from sin, Lord.

I didn't understand, Lord.

I need you, Lord.

I love you, Lord.

You are with me, Lord.[12]

Worship doesn't come easily, even for the redeemed. We are prone to wander and love things we shouldn't. Worship is indeed warfare. Joseph Carroll captures the challenge before us, "Worship is not simple, but it is glorious! I have found … that it is the one thing the enemy will oppose more than anything else…. The one thing he does not want is for you to worship Jesus Christ."[13] Thus, with resolve we must declare, "You have said, 'Seek my face.' My heart says to you, 'Your face, Lord, do I seek'" (Psa. 27:8).

Altar Moments

1. Read Hebrews 11:1–6. What do you learn about faith from these verses? Do you agree that the word "faith" has lost its meaning as defined in Scripture? Was it helpful to identify biblical, saving faith as having content, agreement, and trust?

2. Why does spiritual worship make perfect sense based upon Paul's argument in Romans 12:1–2?

---

12 Ray Ortlund, Twitter post, July 2, 2020, 6:03 a.m., https://twitter.com/rayortlund/status/1278645517501829120.

13 Joseph Carroll, *How to Worship Jesus Christ* (Chicago: Moody Press Edition 1991), 38.

3. *Coram Deo* was mentioned in this chapter. How does this challenge your thinking regarding your personal worship? Consider the following examples:

- Job 1:5
- Read Psalm 73, the account of Asaph's despair, and his recovery through personal worship. How does v. 17 rescue him? What was his resolve at the end of the psalm, vv. 23–28?
- Jesus in Mark 1:35

4. How do you see worship as being a ballast to keep you steady with the demands of life? What hindrances do you face in personal worship? Is there daily time in your life where you are still before the Lord for the purpose of reading the Bible and prayer?

Prayer:

Gracious Heavenly Father, I love You and want to live my life for You this day. Please allow me to pray in the Spirit because You know what I will face today and where to emphasize my prayers. I realize that when I talk to You in prayer that I am talking to the One who is able to do more than I could ask or think. Be glorified in my life and may I make the most of every opportunity.

In Jesus' Name, Amen.

Chapter 5

Flipping the Script on the World's Agenda

"Do not be conformed to this world, but be
transformed by the renewal of your mind, that by
testing you may discern what is the will of God,
what is good and acceptable and perfect."
Romans 12:2

*I*NEVER GET TIRED OF reading the Gospel accounts of those who were transformed by Jesus. Whether a crippled man lowered through the roof by his friends (Mark 2:1–12), or a chief tax collector who climbed into a sycamore tree to see Jesus as he passed by (Luke 19:1–10), or a Gerasene demoniac who lived a tormented life (Mark 5:1–20) — no one was too far gone for Christ's redeeming power. The power of the gospel is seen in transformed lives.

The apostle Paul experienced the transforming power of Jesus one day on the road to Damascus. His conversion and testimony are emphasized in the book of Acts (9:1–19; 22:6–11;

26:12–18). Paul also shared with Timothy, his son in the faith, how God's saving grace changed him forever: "The saying is trustworthy and deserving of full acceptance, that Christ Jesus came into the world to save sinners, of whom I am the foremost. But I received mercy for this reason, that in me, as the foremost, Jesus Christ might display his perfect patience as an example to those who were to believe in him for eternal life" (1 Tim. 1:15, 16). From his experience with the living Christ, we understand why Paul underscored the transforming power of the gospel in Romans 12. It was the good news that changed his life.

Like Paul, believers in Christ now live on the altar as a living sacrifice to God. In this chapter, we move to Romans 12:2 which contains essential truth for our spiritual growth. Paul writes, "Do not be conformed to this world, but be transformed by the renewal of your mind, that by testing you may discern what is the will of God, what is good and acceptable and perfect." We will break down this verse by looking at three key factors for spiritual growth—we are not conformed to this world's system; we are called to new thinking through the renewal of our mind; and we are motivated to discern God's will for our lives.

Not Conformed, but Transformed

Romans 12:2 reminds us that we are sojourners in this world. We are called to live differently. We are not to live in conformity to this world's system but to be continually transformed into the image of Christ. In the vernacular of the day, we are to live in such a way as to "flip the script on the world's agenda." In other words, Romans 12:2 helps us avoid the powerful, dangerous desires generated by loving the world (1 John 2:15–16).

Pressure from This World's System

When Paul said, "Do not be conformed to this world," he is calling believers to resist the pressure to conform to the world's schemes. This world's system with its values, goals, philosophies, and judgments are at odds with God's sovereign reign. The world is a system that is passing away (1 John 2:17) and conflicts with our pursuit of Christ's kingdom (Matt. 6:33). Living for the approval of the world brings compromise in which we are tempted to live off mission.

The world has always sought to exert pressure on the church to conform to its changing and inconsistent standards. One thing that won't be tolerated by the world are exclusive truth claims. This means a "good Christian" is one who "plays fair" with the other sincere religions and worldviews. This requires believers to make concessions and compromise in order to have a seat at the table of legitimacy on the world's stage. Fair play is agreeing that everyone's belief system is of equal value.

Of course, this will never do living under the authority of Christ who said, "I am the way, and the truth, and the life. No one comes to the Father except through me" (John 14:6). We are convinced that Jesus Christ stands as exclusive Savior and Sovereign Lord over all of history. His testimony before Pontius Pilate is a summary of the timeless message given to the world regardless of the century in which one lives. "Then Pilate said to him, 'So you are a king?' Jesus answered, 'You say that I am a king. For this purpose I was born and for this purpose I have come into the world—to bear witness to the truth. Everyone who is of the truth listens to my voice'" (John 18:37). Pilate's sneer of unbelief in response to Jesus captures the world's creed, "What is truth?" (John 18:38).

I am reminded of Erwin Lutzer's conversation with a woman on an airplane. Lutzer recounted the exchange in one of his books:

> I noticed that the woman across the aisle was wearing a cross necklace. Hoping to stimulate discussion, I said, "Thanks for wearing that cross. We do have a wonderful Savior, don't we?" She rolled her eyes and responded, "Well, I don't think of the cross like you do. Just look at this." She showed me that beneath the cross was the Jewish Star of David, and beneath that was a trinket that symbolized the Hindu god Om. "I'm in social work," she told me. "I've discovered that people find God in different ways. Christianity is but one path to the divine."[1]

No doubt, this woman would have received a hearty "amen" from many captivated by the world's system. Oprah Winfrey exemplifies this sentiment when she said, "One of the biggest mistakes humans make is to believe there is only one way. Actually, there are many diverse paths leading to what you call God."[2]

This kind of resistance to the exclusive claims of Jesus Christ is promised in the New Testament. The apostles, while facing

---

1   Erwin Lutzer, *Ten Lies about God and How You Might Already Be Deceived* (Nashville: Word Publishing, 2000), 24.

2   LaTonya Taylor, "The Church of O," *Christianity Today*, accessed June 18, 2021, https://www.christianitytoday.com/ct/2002/april1/church-oprah-winfrey.html.

persecution, proclaimed, "There is no other name under heaven given among men by which we must be saved" (Acts 4:12). The message of the cross confronts the religious, exposes our sin, calls for repentance, and claims to be the only way to God. And it is upon these truth claims that Christians are called to stand. Our identity is in Jesus Christ, and we gladly follow Him. We resist conformity to the world when we stand on His truth.

A Daunting Task at Times

Yet, flipping the script on the world's agenda can be a daunting task. R. Kent Hughes recognized the challenge when he wrote, "Sometimes it is difficult to know when we are conforming because there are many good things in the world."[3] So, we always need to examine what is an excellent use of our time and resources to ensure that we are investing them according to the values of God's kingdom.

There is another challenge, as well. When Christians think about not conforming to this world, often there is a temptation to list things that are forbidden as a statement of our nonconformity. But lists of forbidden behaviors vary among believers and are often driven by cultural influences. That being the case, our lists always seem to miss the point. Inevitably, they breed a pharisaical attitude. Instead, as our consciences are informed by the Word of God, we must stop doing certain things because they are sinful and hinder our walk with Christ. Yet, there should be

---

3   R. Kent Hughes, *Romans: Righteousness from Heaven* in *Preaching the Word* (Wheaton: Crossway Books, 1991), 215, Logos Bible Software.

love and liberty among believers as we work out these matters in our lives.

At the heart of not conforming to this world is the necessity for believers to put off sin in their lives and to put on the Lord Jesus Christ. Paul's statement in Ephesians 4:20–24 serves as a helpful commentary in navigating the shoals of this world's agenda by putting off our old self and being "renewed in the spirit of [our] minds, and to put on the new self, created after the likeness of God in true righteousness and holiness."

These verses sound very similar to Romans 12:1–2. They remind us of our need to resist conformity to the world's objectives and to pursue the renewal of our minds by the power of the gospel.

A Renewed Mind: New Thinking for a New Life

Timothy Lane and Paul Tripp in their helpful book, *How People Change*, introduce their readers to a man and his wife, Phil and Ellie. Phil was familiar with Scripture and systematic theology and boasted of an extensive library of biblical commentaries by the "who's who" of theological writers. Yet, even with this impressive spiritual repertoire, there was something wrong with Phil's life. Lane and Tripp wrote, "If you were to turn from Phil's library and watch the video of his life, you would see a very different man."[4]

Phil gave the appearance that all was in order: "He had the theological dexterity of a gymnast, but he lived like a relational

---

4   Timothy Lane and Paul Tripp, *How People Change* (Greensboro: New Growth Press, 2008), 1.

paraplegic."[5] His marriage, while outwardly portraying health, was really on a lifeline because of his harsh and impatient responses to his wife. His relationship with his children was distant at best. He was not satisfied with his job, and one could assume that he was in a constant scrimmage with his boss(es). What was unstable in these areas was also true of his church life, where he had joined his fourth church in three decades. Despite his outward persona of being a mature believer, his problems siphoned off time for meaningful ministry. Love, grace, and joy were not the fruit of Phil's life.

From the outside, no one would have guessed this disparity in his life. This seemed to add to Ellie's frustration with the church. Because no one understood what Phil was really like, Ellie had to fight bitterness. When things began to unravel prompting Ellie and Phil to finally pursue counseling, the counselor observed, "They had given extensive history of their situation, yet there was little or no reference to God. Here was a theological man and his believing wife, yet their life story was utterly godless."[6]

Lane and Tripp called this discrepancy "The Gospel Gap,"[7] which they defined as "a vast gap in our grasp of the gospel. It subverts our identity as Christians and our understanding of the present work of God. This gap undermines every relationship in our lives, every decision we make, and every attempt to minister to others. Yet we live blindly, as if the hole were not there."[8]

---

5   Ibid.
6   Ibid, 2.
7   Ibid, 1.
8   Ibid.

Romans 12:1–2 provides insight into how the gap is closed between what we know and how we live. Paul's admonition is to "be transformed by the renewal of your mind" (v. 2). As our minds are renewed by God's truth, we see things that God wants to change in our lives. Through the mercies of God found in Christ, we are given new eyes to see what must change and now have His power to makes changes.

The renewal process is not for the faint of heart. Sometimes, change comes slowly, and it seems that nothing drags more stubbornly than our failures. Yet, this is the path of continual growth and transformation that leads to true change for the glory of God.

Demystifying the Will of God

Another blessing that comes from the Altar Life described in Romans 12 is the ability to know and do the will of God. Paul closes verse 2 with one of the great outcomes of a transformed life, namely the ability to "prove what the will of God is, that which is good and acceptable and perfect" (v. 2). This promise demystifies God's will for every believer. I admit that we will not always know in the clearest terms every specific decision we are to make. God's will is often mysterious. However, in this statement, Paul gives tremendous clarity for the believer to live in confidence of God's pleasure and direction over his or her life.

Conversations about the will of God can quickly become confusing, because the distinction between God's sovereign will and God's commanded will are often blurred. Yet, making this distinction is vital to navigating the tensions in Scripture. How are we to understand the difference between God's sovereign will and His commanded will? Which one is referenced in Romans 12:2?

God's Sovereign Will

Early in the Bible, we discover that God is sovereign. He is a God of order who possesses all power and rules all things. He gives directives and commands.[9] He rules the universe with purpose and a predetermined plan that all things will be brought into complete submission to Christ. We find this expressed powerfully in Paul's letter to the Philippians: "That at the name of Jesus every knee should bow … and every tongue confess that Jesus Christ is Lord, to the glory of God the Father" (Phil. 2:10–11).

God has revealed that He indeed has a sovereign plan that is centered on the redeeming work of His Son, the Lord Jesus Christ. Through Christ, He will unite all things in the universe (1 Cor. 15:24–28). This is an amazing comfort in a world groaning under the weight of untold sorrow. God has a sovereign plan, and it will be fulfilled in time.

While we know that God has a sovereign plan for the world and everything in it, we don't know the specific details of it. In Deuteronomy we find that "the secret things belong to the Lord our God, but the things that are revealed belong to us and to our children forever, that we may do all the words of this law" (Deut.

---

9   In the Creation account of Genesis 1, God is mentioned 32 times in 31 verses. In this chapter, He "created," "said," "saw," "separated," "called," "made," and "blessed." With each creative act, the refrain of the narrative was that it was good and on the sixth day with the creation of man, "It was very good" (v. 31).

29:29). There are some things that we will never know concerning how God works in the drama of history, nor do we know the details of how He will bring history to a close. But we know that He will! We don't know when Christ will return, but we know God's sovereign plan is that He will return and every eye will see him (Rev. 1:7).

God's Commanded Will

In contrast, God's commanded will speaks to something we can know specifically, because it has been revealed in Scripture. This is what Paul means when he writes in Romans 12:2 that believers are to test and discern "the will of God." We are to bring God's revelation to bear on the decisions of our lives. The will of God is described in beautiful terms as that which is "good and acceptable and perfect," (Rom. 12:2) which is encouraging to every believer in Christ and should fuel our pursuit of knowing God's revealed will. Furthermore, the pursuit of God's will should be something we fully embrace, yielding great assurance that we are fulfilling the purposes for which we were created.

But unfortunately, for many Christians, the concept of knowing the will of God is a point of confusion, doubt, and fear. Instead of the principles and precepts of God's Word illuminating the path of their decision-making, many believers grope in darkness, living off the husks of their own instincts.

Paul's command to discern God's will should be our life's quest. The use of the Greek word *dokimázō* in verse 2 suggests a deliberate focus on knowing God's revealed will that should characterize the believer's life. The word is translated "prove"

(NASB) or "discern" (ESV) and refers to testing something to establish its value. It has the idea of testing and approving something that involves more than common sense. Using this word here in verse 2 suggests a treasuring of something that is valuable and true. This is how Paul describes the believer's motivation to pursue and to understand God's will.

A common question asked by many Christians is, "How do I know God's will for my life?" To answer that question, a believer must look at what God commands. This is at the heart of what Paul is urging in Romans 12:2. Testing and discerning the will of God is a dynamic process that brings together the light of God's Word with the relationships, opportunities, desires, and circumstances of our lives.

In surveying the New Testament, I was amazed at the many references to the will of God as the focal point for Christian living. God's revealed will is a subject that requires more study than our current discourse can afford. But, for the purposes of our discussion, let's look at a few Scripture references and see how these commands guide us in knowing and doing God's will.

Jesus was not silent about seeking and obeying the will of God. He said in Matthew 7:21, "Not everyone who says to me, 'Lord, Lord,' will enter the kingdom of heaven, but the one who does the will of my Father who is in heaven." This is a disturbing statement for religious people who are trusting in their religiosity. This verse, of course, is found in the Sermon on the Mount which, in part, dismantles the self-righteous attitudes and practices of the Pharisees. Jesus warned that religious activity will not usher a person into the kingdom of heaven, yet He pointed the way to His kingdom by stating that it is "the one who does the will of my Father who is in heaven." The one who humbly surrenders his life to Christ and His commands and, thus, walks by faith in Him is the one who does the will of the Father.

Paul urged the Ephesians, "Therefore do not be foolish, but understand what the will of the Lord is" (Eph. 5:17). This is a warning to believers not to fritter away opportunities to serve Christ. Pursuing God's will brings an intensity to life that requires focus in order to capitalize on the opportunities of service that God gives us. Missionary David Brainerd exemplified such resolve in the throes of a difficult life, when he said, "May I never loiter in my heavenly journey."[10] To loiter means "to stand or wait around idly or without apparent purpose." Brainerd did not want to loaf in his service to Christ, and we should not do so either.

Paul's straightforwardness with the Thessalonians was refreshing, when he wrote, "For this is the will of God, your sanctification: that you abstain from sexual immorality" (1 Thess. 4:3). This command clarifies much, doesn't it? This verse is not ambiguous about how I am to live in this world regarding sexual purity. Also, it is God's will for me, and every believer, to be sanctified, conformed to the image of Christ (Rom. 8:29). My life is to be an ongoing process of this pursuit.

Furthermore, Paul becomes more specific about God's will and sanctification when he says, "that you abstain from sexual immorality." The Greek word used here is *porneía*, which is the

---

10 David Brainerd, *The Diary and Journal of David Brainerd* (Carlisle, PA: The Banner of Truth Trust, 2007), 76.

root word for pornography. This term describes any sexual behavior outside of marriage. Sexual expression is a glorious gift
of God which is to be enjoyed within the confines of what the
writer of Hebrews called "the marriage bed" (Heb. 13:4). God's
will for every believer is to walk in sexual purity. God has not
been cryptic concerning His commanded will. When we read
such commands in the New Testament, properly interpreted, we
can know God's will.

How Do We Apply This?

Years ago, John MacArthur wrote a book, *Found: God's Will*, in
which he presents several basic questions for one seeking to find
God's direction and purpose for his or her life. The questions
could be summarized in this way:

> Am I in a saving relationship with Jesus Christ?
>
> Am I seeking to be filled with the Holy Spirit?
>
> Am I serious about my sanctification?
>
> Am I submissive to the counsel of God's Word and
> the authorities in my life?
>
> Am I embracing the suffering and trials that come
> as I follow Christ?[11]

MacArthur's premise is that if the answer to these questions
is in the affirmative, if these basic areas of the Christian life are
being followed and obeyed, then MacArthur's counsel here is,

---

11 John MacArthur, *Found: God's Will, Find the Direction and Purpose God Wants
for Your Life* (Colorado Springs: David C. Cook, 2012), 67. These questions follow the chapter themes of the book.

"Do whatever you want!"[12] Far from reckless, this seems to be the freedom that accompanies many references to the commanded will of God in the New Testament.

We are not always going to find specifics for the decisions we face. Decisions like who to marry? What vocation to pursue? Should I go to the mission field or the pastorate? Where should I attend college? Should I purchase this car or house or computer? Should I move to such-and-such city? But the Word of God gives guidance that we can bring to bear in our pursuit of God's will for our lives. Discerning the will of God is a dynamic process that brings the light and authority of Scripture to bear upon the details of life.

Boice offers helpful guidance about a Christian's freedom to make decisions. "We may not know what that specific will is and we do not need to be under pressure to 'discover' it, fearing that if we miss it, somehow we will be doomed to a life outside the center of God's will. We are free to make decisions with what light and wisdom we possess."[13]

Life on the Altar, as Paul is describing in Romans 12:1–2, is presenting ourselves to God who is worthy of our greatest devotion. As our minds are renewed, we decline conformity with this world in exchange for transformation through the power of the gospel. The Christian life is not without trial. We can expect to labor in determining the details and decisions before us. But there is no better life to live. Thus, Paul describes the will of God

12 Ibid, 68.
13 Boice, *Romans*, 1557.

for the believer as that which "is good and acceptable and perfect" (Rom. 12:2b).

Altar Moments

1. Several accounts from the Gospels were mentioned in this chapter of Jesus' transforming power in people's lives. Look at Mark 2:1–12; Mark 5:1–20; and Luke 19:1–10. How do these passages inform us about people's problems and the power of Christ? When you read the Gospels, what is your favorite encounter of Jesus? Why is it meaningful to you?

2. In the section on discerning the will of God, are the questions used from MacArthur's book helpful? If faced with a major decision in your life, how would the application of Romans 12:2 help you in discerning the will of the Lord?

Prayer:

"Father, you're certainly honored when we work hard to make good plans in keeping with our understanding of the Scriptures. It's important for us to seek and heed the wise, prayerful counsel of good and godly friends.

But help us to live with more confidence that Jesus is the Good Shepherd, not a consulting partner; a very present Lord, not an absentee landlord; the reigning King, not an impotent bystander.

Because of Jesus, I'm confident your will is being done, on earth as it is in heaven. I pray in his exalted name. Amen."[14]

---

14 Scotty Smith, *Everyday Prayers: 365 Days to a Gospel-Centered Faith* (Grand Rapids: Baker Books, 2011), location 2140, Kindle edition.

Part 2

Presenting Ourselves to God in Body Life

*A*s WE COME TO Part 2 of the book, my aim is to trace Paul's transition from presenting ourselves to God as living sacrifices to presenting ourselves to a local body of believers. I am not suggesting that we ever leave the altar for something else, only that altar life necessarily leads to life in a local church. When we taste of the mercies of God found in Jesus Christ, we begin to love what He loves. Nothing is clearer from the New Testament than Christ's love for His church (Eph. 5:25).

The next four chapters will be based primarily on Romans 12:3–8, which addresses life in the body of Christ:

> **For by the grace given to me I say to everyone among you not to think of himself more highly than he ought to think, but to think with sober judgment, each according to the measure of faith that God has assigned. For as in one body we have many members, and the members do not all have the same function, so we, though many, are one body in Christ, and individually members one of another. Having gifts that differ according to the grace given to us, let us use them: if prophecy, in proportion to our faith; if service, in our serving; the one who teaches, in his teaching; the one who exhorts, in his exhortation; the one who contributes, in generosity; the one who leads, with zeal; the one who does acts of mercy, with cheerfulness.**

In chapter 6, we'll show how we are redeemed to live our lives in a spiritual family called a local church. In chapter 7, we'll give examples of ways the New Testament presents "Body Life," specifically the picture of love and affection for one another. This flows to chapter 8, where we will take a close look at the "one another" statements in the New Testament. Chapter 9 will conclude Part Two with a challenge regarding spiritual gifts.

Chapter 6

Redeemed to Live Life in a Family

"Therefore, as God's chosen people, holy and dearly loved, clothe yourselves with compassion, kindness, humility, gentleness and patience. Bear with each other and forgive one another if any of you has a grievance against someone. Forgive as the Lord forgave you." Colossians 3:12–13

WHEN I WAS A freshman in high school, I had a football coach who was intense, *very* intense. His intensity was especially evident with players he didn't like, players like me. At least, that was true my freshman year which was a proving ground in his mind. Thankfully, I survived Coach's wrath that first season which led to an improved status for my future years of high school.

Coach had a mustache that resembled the look of a proverbial Viking on a conquest. He was the kind of man who, during his tour-of-duty in Vietnam, spent his free time killing water buffalos with his .50 caliber machine gun. In the strangest of contrasts, school administrators assigned him to teach driver's education. I will always remember how he greeted the class as he looked at us that first day: "Well," he scoffed, "this isn't the freshman class at Harvard." That was certainly an accurate assessment!

I remember Coach's greeting every time I read the apostle Paul's charge to the Corinthian church:

> **For consider your calling, brothers: not many of you were wise according to worldly standards, not many were powerful, not many were of noble birth. But God chose what is foolish in the world to shame the wise; God chose what is weak in the world to shame the strong; God chose what is low and despised in the world, even things that are not, to bring to nothing things that are, so that no human being might boast in the presence of God. (1 Cor. 1:26–29)**

Paul was saying to the Corinthians, and to us, "Notice, your gathering is not made up of the 'movers and shakers' of the culture. Your curriculum vitae is not very impressive in the world's eyes, but that's okay. It's okay because the church is not about you. You don't make it great. The church is about showcasing God's grace and glory through the redeeming work of Jesus Christ. He is great, and the gathering of the church will always be about Him." What Paul said to the Corinthians, he also applied to himself as he expressed later in this same letter, "For I am the least of the apostles, unworthy to be called an apostle, because I persecuted the church of God" (1 Cor. 15:9).

When Paul reflected on the makeup of the church, he didn't congratulate them on their achievements or their resumes. Rather, he pointed out that "God chose what is foolish in the world to shame the wise; God chose what is weak in the world to shame the strong" (1 Cor. 1:27). This emphasis on humility is crucial to our understanding of New Testament teaching about the local church and should inform our expectations and involvement in the church that we attend.

Learning to Walk in Humility

Paul's description of believers from God's perspective in 1 Corinthians should foster humility in us all. Christians are often called foolish and weak according to this world's system for the purpose of displaying God's wisdom and strength. Not surprisingly, Paul challenges believers in Romans 12 to pursue humility in our relationships with others: "For by the grace given to me I say to everyone among you not to think of himself more highly than he ought to think, but to think with sober judgment, each according to the measure of faith that God has assigned" (v. 3). Our motivation for humility inside and outside the church should be empowered by a conscious awareness of God's grace given to each one of us in Christ.

Think of the problems that would be resolved in this world and in the church if followers of Christ lived this way. We know that this world is shot through with the vestiges of pride. I once read that pride grows in the human heart like lard on a pig. The roots of pride run deep in the human story, and its viscous foliage shows itself with little effort. We don't have to work hard for pride to be manifested in our lives. Even noble and good things can become soured by this pernicious sin. Pride flows freely from our fallen hearts. Tracing its roots is not difficult. All we need is to look back to Eden where Adam and Eve took of the forbidden fruit and catapulted the human family into the misery we presently know. Since then, we all contribute to the groaning of this creation when we think of ourselves more highly than we ought and deny that we need God.

Throughout Scripture, God records what He thinks about pride. In the book of Proverbs, we read that God abominates "haughty eyes" (Prov. 6:17), and we are warned that "pride goes before destruction, and a haughty spirit before stumbling" (Prov. 16:18 NASB). Jesus taught that pride came forth from the human heart (Mark 7:15). The apostle James asserted that "God opposes the proud but gives grace to the humble" (Jas. 4:6). The word "opposes" in this text describes God's ongoing hatred and opposition to pride. The apostle John referenced "the boastful pride of life" (1 John 2:16) in his warning to believers against loving this present world system.

We should be concerned at how pride shows itself in our lives. How it often is the *modus operandi* in the way to get things done. If we are to resist conformity to the world, like we are instructed to do in Romans 12:2, then one of the first places to begin is in the pursuit of humility. John MacArthur's observations ring true when he wrote, "Obsession with self is not only deemed acceptable nowadays, it is considered normal behavior.

Our culture has made pride a virtue and humility a weakness."[1] The church is called to display true humility that begins in our relationships within the body of Christ.

One of the most effective pride busters available is a faithful relationship with a church family. A believer's involvement in a local body declares and demonstrates a level of humility. I am very aware that the opposite is true, namely that church involvement can breed self-righteousness that is appalling. Unfortunately, church history is littered with the prideful witness of God's people. However, what God's people should communicate is that we are gathered to say collectively, "I'm needy. I need Jesus Christ. I need His Word in my life. I need the fellowship of other believers to be sharpened, strengthened, and challenged. I am aligning myself with God's people who will live with Him forever and ever."

I fear many may take access to church life for granted. My travels in East Asia have taken me into the gatherings of many house churches. These believers overcome many difficulties just to gather. From arrests to family pressures to work schedules, there is nothing convenient about church life for believers in East Asia. They meet because they are desperate for God and needy for each other. I once preached a Sunday gathering in a 12 x 20 room in which the brothers and sisters were packed shoulder-to-shoulder. The temperature was over 90 degrees with no air conditioning. Their joy was contagious; their singing, while in Chinese, was the sweetest sound I've ever heard in a worship

---

1   John MacArthur, "The Humility of Love," *Grace to You*, accessed January 10, 2021, https://www.gty.org/library/blog/B170109/.

service. As I preached on the second coming from 1 Thessalonians 4:13–18, the spiritual hunger of that gathering was indescribable. I left knowing that I had been privileged to one of the greatest experiences a believer could have. We need reminders not to take Body Life for granted. Specifically, how can faithfulness to a local church help us pursue humility in our walk with Christ?

Giving of Ourselves to Others

First, church life gives us an opportunity to give of ourselves to others. Followers of Christ are called to serve one another. In John 13, Jesus washed the feet of His disciples, and then commanded them to go and do likewise. This seems to raise the question for our personal consideration: "Whose feet am I washing on a regular basis?" If we would have eyes to see the opportunities around us, church life can place us on the front lines of service to others, both in the church and to those outside. Jesus also said in the Upper Room, "By this all people will know that you are my disciples, if you have love for one another" (John 13:35). We will provide detailed application in Chapter 8 of this book with a look at what it means to obey the "one another" commands of the New Testament. There are over thirty such commands given to us for the purpose of giving ourselves to others.

Receiving from Others

Secondly, each believer, including me, has needs in his life that cannot be met on one's own. One of the strong pulls of pride is for us to say to ourselves, "I don't need church. I can meet my own spiritual needs in my own way." We must do battle with those kinds of thoughts, because they are contrary to the instruction of God's Word which warns us against the neglect of the church gathering (Heb. 10:25). We need the accountability and the sharpening that can only come through a committed membership in a local church. We all have blind spots, sins, and weaknesses in our lives that we simply cannot see. Humility acknowledges freely that I need to receive from others what I lack as an important part of my spiritual growth. How do we get the most out of the grace afforded to us in belonging to a church family?

Paul emphasizes in Romans 12:3 the importance of putting pride to death in our hearts. Identifying pride is an elusive endeavor because it can color many things about us. Flying under our spiritual radar, pride is a stealth sin that can wreak havoc before we identify it. With such a formidable struggle before each of us, what hope do we have of putting off pride and putting on humility? Thankfully, the counsel of God's Word is not silent on how we can recognize pride. God's grace comes to us for this battle through establishing holy habits, or spiritual disciplines, in our lives. Consider with me how one of those spiritual disciplines, church membership, can bring forth the fruit of humility.

Church Life as a Spiritual Discipline

Commitment to church life is waning in our culture. Bill Gates speaks for many when he said in a *Time* magazine interview nearly twenty-five years ago, "Just in terms of allocation of time resources, religion is not very efficient. There's a lot more I could be doing on Sunday morning."[2] His words were a harbinger of a decline in church attendance throughout the United States. I can understand an unbeliever questioning the value of church life, and in the end saying, as Bill Gates did, "No thanks." But for the follower of Christ, we are called to unite with a local fellowship for the purpose of living the Christian life together. This is not a suggestion; it is a matter of obedience.

A recent Gallup poll bears witness to the mindset expressed by Gates, as American church membership has fallen below the majority for the first time. The poll followed church membership over the last 80 years with a peak of 76% following World War II, but the poll noted a sharp decline in the last twenty years to 47%. This is the first-time church attendance has fallen below 50% in the United States.[3]

When I read statistics like this, my first take is that this poll covered all religions, not just Christianity, and indicates a secular trend in American culture. However, my allegiance is not to religion but to the gospel. My heartbreak over the church's decline in our culture is not driven by Gallup numbers or a desire to keep the club going as if it were a civic organization. My mourning is for the state of the church. Indeed, the times are desperate for a move of God. But the church is not, and that is evidenced by our neglect of Body Life. When we forsake the gathering of the church, we forfeit the benefits of the preaching of God's

---

2 Walter Isaacson, "In Search of the Real Bill Gates," *Time*, accessed February 4, 2021, http://content.time.com/time/magazine/article/0,9171,1120657-8,00.html.
3 Jeffrey M. Jones, "U.S. Church Membership Falls Below Majority for First Time," *Gallup*, accessed March 29, 2021, https://news.gallup.com/poll/341963/church-membership-falls-below-majority-first-time.aspx.

Word, prayer, fellowship, encouragement, and many other gifts God has for those who love Him. If Christians don't prioritize church life, why would we expect anything but decline?

Seeing your church family as a priority is an important step in the right direction. Paul wrote to Timothy, "Train yourself for godliness" (1 Tim. 4:7). The Greek word *gumnázō* is translated "train" in the ESV. This word influenced the forming of the English word "gymnasium." Paul's challenge and word picture are clear. Believers are to exercise and train themselves for the purpose of growing in the grace and knowledge of the Lord Jesus Christ. "Holy sweat"[4] is required, again, not to earn salvation, but for the rigor of living for Jesus in this world. We find in Scripture such spiritual disciplines as: biblical intake, prayer, worship, evangelism, serving, stewardship, fasting, and church life. This is not an exhaustive list but representative of basic commitments believers should embrace to grow in their faith.

As we face the world, our flesh, and the evil one, God has given to us spiritual disciplines to help us walk in humility. One of the most important exercises in the Christian life is the spiritual discipline of regularly, consistently gathering with a local body of believers. I include church life among the list of spiritual disciplines because believers are called to be meaningfully connected to a local church, and this requires discipline. God's plan for us is life lived in a church family where we learn to walk in love and humility as we seek God's kingdom together.

---

4   R. Kent Hughes, *Disciplines of a Godly Man,* 10th Anniversary Edition (Wheaton: Crossway, 2001), 80, Kindle edition. In addition to Hughes' work, Donald S. Whitney's *Spiritual Disciplines for the Christian Life* (Colorado Springs: NavPress, 2014) has been extremely helpful in my study of spiritual disciplines.

The book of Acts captures a beautiful picture of church life (Acts 2:42–47). In context, the apostle Peter had just preached on the day of Pentecost and the Holy Spirit had come in fulfillment of the promise given by Jesus (John 14:15–17). As a result of the gospel preached, 3,000 people came to faith in Jesus on that day. Luke described this glorious manifestation of God's presence with His people. From this account in Acts 2, we observe a band of new believers gathered because of their common bond in Christ. The practice of the early church is very instructive. What were they doing?

First, they worshiped together. These new believers were in "awe" of God's presence and the work He was doing among them (v. 43). They were "praising God" as the new covenant promises were being received through Jesus. The entire city of Jerusalem was experiencing a supernatural visitation, and the Word of God was proclaimed. As a result, "The Lord added to their number day by day those who were being saved" (v. 47).

Second, they received instruction together. The text says, "They devoted themselves to the apostles' teaching" (v. 42). From the beginning, Christianity has emphasized the importance of teaching and preaching God's Word when the church is gathered. The spiritual hunger and devotion of these new believers is convicting. The description of the early church in Acts 2 could be summarized as a group of believers, "Lost in wonder, love, and praise."[5] Could our church gatherings be described in these terms? Are we devoted to the Word of God in this way?

---

5   Charles Wesley, "Love Divine, All Loves Excelling," pubic domain.

Charles Spurgeon wrote of the spiritual lethargy of his day. "Everywhere there is apathy. Nobody cares whether that which is preached is true or false. A sermon is a sermon whatever the subject; only the shorter it is the better."[6] I fear that this sounds all too familiar in many church gatherings today.

Third, they shared fellowship together (v. 42). Their new commitment to follow Christ would cost them, and they needed each other for spiritual support, as well as for practical needs. They prayed together, and they ate together. Luke describes the intimacy of their relationship with one another: "And all who believed were together and had all things in common. And they were selling their possessions and belongings and distributing the proceeds to all, as any had need. And day by day, attending the temple together and breaking bread in their homes, they received their food with glad and generous hearts" (Acts 2:44–46).

Lastly, the early church in Acts 2 expressed themselves through personal ministry. In reading this account, you get the impression that these early believers couldn't have made it without one another. This is what I long for in my church and in yours. Such an expression is best given through a church walking in humility and love for the glory of Christ. Has your heart grown cold to church life? Have you been burned in a church conflict? Do you have memories that are not good? Maybe you have just drifted away from church life for any number of reasons? Maybe you agree with Bill Gates and believe you could spend your time better doing something else?

---

6   Charles Spurgeon, *The Sword and the Trowel* (London: Passmore & Alabaster, 1888), iii.

I understand the pull, but I would encourage you to return to the local church. It's not because we are trying to keep the club open or avoid foreclosure, or because it's my job as a pastor. The reason every believer should be in a local church is because God has purposed to display His glory through the church where the members are radically committed to the Lord and to one another. From the beginning of the new covenant era until now, the local church is the epicenter of God's kingdom purposes. And it is where believers need to give their best to one another and, above all, to Christ.

Avoiding Spiritual Implosion

I have always been fascinated at how engineers can bring down old, unwanted buildings in the middle of a city skyline. One thing is for sure in these projects, the engineers are not haphazard in the placement of the explosives. They want the building to implode, not explode. The goal is to have the building collapse and fall straight down, as opposed to an explosion that would send shrapnel into the city.

Implosion describes an intense collapse inward and is the method of destruction when it comes to bringing down unwanted buildings. While it may be helpful in removing old buildings, implosion in our spiritual lives is devastating. When a believer spiritually implodes, there is a violent collapse inward that causes the heart to harden, which in turn, makes it difficult to receive truth or serve the Lord with joy.

Spiritual implosion begins in the secret place of the heart. The Evil One's strategy is to get us alone and then beat the life out of us. Our local church is God's answer to the assassin's plot. We need the ministry that can only come through a full immersion in a local church family. It is within the confines of gathered believers that we can worship, receive instruction, fellowship, and give of ourselves in personal ministry.

Our commitment to our local church family is not dictated by convenience. We understand that faithfulness to Christ means showing up in the Body even when life is hard. I will never forget the example of one member in our FBCG family who some years ago was on the front page of *The Advocate*, the major newspaper serving the Baton Rouge area. The story along with his picture implicated him in a crime. It was a humiliating and devastating article that brought embarrassment to him and his family. As the weekend came, he could have made every excuse in the world to avoid coming to church, but he didn't. Sunday came, and he took his place among his church family reminding us of our need for God's grace. In the days that followed this brother walked through the necessary process with integrity and humility and has been faithful to serve the Lord since being fully exonerated.

Embracing the Frustrations and Pain in the Family of God

We all know that the church is not a perfect place. In fact, it is a flawed gathering. It has been said many times that the church is like Noah's ark—the stench inside would be unbearable if it weren't for the storm outside. If you have been in a church for very long, you know it is true. Sometimes, we smell, and yes, the world is stormy. However, this is the wonder of God's mystery. He has chosen the weakness and the foolishness inside the church to confound the world's thinking.

When we were adopting our youngest daughter from China, part of the pre-adoption curriculum was to view a video entitled, "Eyes Wide Open." The video was an effort to prepare parents for possible difficulties that they may face with the new child in their family. As intended, the material was sobering yet helpful in setting expectations for a full range of possibilities. The same is true with life in a local church. We need eyes wide open to difficulties, but that is not the whole story. We are not to live focused on the negative. We are not to be like those people described by the English poet Thomas Hardy who are brought into a beautiful meadow and first point to a manure pile. God intends for His church to be an oasis of grace for His people and a witness of light to this world. Church life is to be a respite from the blows of life. While challenging, church relationships and experiences have filled my life with a thousand joys. I have come to see over-and-over that God's people were redeemed to live life in such a family and that enduring any bumps and scrapes with my fellow believers is worth it all.

I have experienced the best and worst of church life. There have been times when life in the Body has been anything but a respite or an oasis. On my first Sunday as pastor of First Baptist Church Gonzales, 120 people left the fellowship to start another church across town. I wasn't the cause of their exodus. The church had been a warring congregation for some time and best described by Jesus in these words, "For from now on in one house there will be five divided, three against two and two against three" (Luke 12:52). There were times in my early years that I felt I was pastoring three churches gathered under one roof.

Considering the troubled background of the church, no doubt some who left on that first Sunday considered that the new pastor was 28 years old and was walking into a spiritual warzone. The consensus seemed to be that there was no way in which I was going to right this ship. They were certainly correct. Without the Lord, the church would not have survived. I've learned in the pastorate that no one loves the church more than Christ, and my focus in ministry is to do what He has commanded me to do—preach the Word and love His people.

So, I am quite aware of the good, the bad, and the ugly of church life. In some seasons, circumstances were extremely difficult and challenging. Honestly, it was hard to reconcile the exalted claims of the church in the New Testament with the pain of the pastorate. There have been times in ministry when I have been tempted to move to Montana and get a shift at McDonald's. However, I have found that persevering through difficulties in Body Life have brought some of the richest blessings I have ever known as a believer. Jesus really is sovereign over His church. He really walks among His lampstand (Rev. 1:13; 2:1). Such trials are a call to humble myself before the Lord, to confess my sin (especially pride), to search the Scripture for insight, to receive counsel from others, and perhaps most difficult of all, to wait on God to move.

May we never think of ourselves more highly than we ought. God's intention for His children is to live in the context of a local church, in a family, where we allow ourselves to be known and where we get to know others. It is here that we learn to walk in love and humility, as we seek God's kingdom together.

Altar Moments

1. Why do you think the apostle Paul begins with a call for humility as he introduces Body Life in Romans 12:3–8?

2. When you think of church life, do you think of it as an "oasis of grace" or a "respite" from the storms of life? Why or why not? Does the analogy of the church resembling Noah's ark seem helpful in setting expectations?

3. What are some of the best memories you have in your local church? Make a list of memories for which you are thankful. Contact members in your church family who have impacted your life and express your gratitude.

Prayer:

Dear Lord,

By the truth of Your Word, and the power of Your Spirit, and the ministry of Your church, revive Your people in our generation. May the message of the cross be proclaimed and may Your grace run to needy hearts. I present myself to You as a living sacrifice and ask that:

My love for You be first over all things,

My love for others be without question,

My growth be evidenced by all,

My witness be compelling,

My words reveal that I have been with You,

My heart perseveres in all things until I see You. In Jesus' Name, Amen.

Chapter 7

Family Affection

"And there was much weeping on the part of all;
they embraced Paul and kissed him."
Acts 20:37—Paul's departure from
the Ephesian Elders at Miletus

ONE OF THE MOST beautiful metaphors of church life in
the New Testament is that of a close-knit family. Families
are to model the love of Christ and relay the truth from one generation to another. We know from experience and history that
neither the family nor the church is perfect. We are redeemed
sinners being conformed into the image of our Savior. Like any
family tree, we don't have to look very far to find imperfections
in the church. It's as easy as a gaze in the mirror. Nevertheless,
each church exists to make known the wonder of God's grace
found in Jesus Christ, and this is seen prominently through
healthy, loving relationships.

In a pastoral effort to promote these kinds of relationships in
our church, I give a 90-Day Challenge on a regular basis to our

corporate worship gathering. Basically, the 90-Day Challenge is an invitation to those visiting to attend for three months. No pressure, just come. It's difficult to assess a church in one visit. For some looking for a church, the differences from previous church experiences and expectations can be overpowering. Consequently, many are "one and done" in their church attendance and bail out prematurely. We cannot treat a search for a church like a drive-through at a fast-food restaurant. We need time to pray and think about a number of things. Over the course of the 90 days, I urge those who are willing to take the challenge to ask several questions.

The first question is, "Am I learning more about the Bible here? Is the Bible opened, read, preached, taught, and applied faithfully?" Asking this helps a person to consider the church's commitment to the Scriptures. There are disturbing trends in contemporary Christianity. One of the worst is a neglect of biblical intake in the body. Many pastors exacerbate the problem by neglecting biblical exposition in favor of giving cultural analysis, offering self-help tips, and catering to perceived needs of the congregation. Without apology, we want to model a thoroughly biblical ministry that emphasizes hearing, reading, studying, memorizing, meditating, and obeying the Word of God (1 Tim. 4:6–16). Ultimately, the Bible is the timeless message that we are charged to communicate.

A second question points to the gospel—is the message of this church pointing me to a saving relationship with Christ? We never graduate from the gospel; it is the message of the ages. When Paul preached in Athens he declared, "The times of ignorance God overlooked, but now he commands all people everywhere to repent" (Acts 17:30). When considering a fellowship of believers, one should ask, "Is the gospel message presented clearly?"

A third question we encourage is, "Do I see love modeled in the relationships of this church?" This question challenges our members, as well as the visitor. Are we a people who love as Jesus commanded? We believe this question can lead to answers that give clarity. This third question moves us to the theme of this chapter on family affection in the body of Christ.

Following the progression of Romans 12, we see that Life on the Altar leads to life in the body of Christ. Paul writes, "For as in one body we have many members, and the members do not all have the same function, so we, though many, are one body in Christ, and individually members one of another" (Rom. 12:4–5). Paul emphasizes the unity of believers as being "one body." He also points to the diversity with reference to "many members." How is the church with many members to function and to relate to one another?

First Love, Then Hate

Paul begins with love in Romans 12:9 when he writes, "Let love be genuine." This is not surprising because love (*agape*) is always at the top of the list of Christian virtues. Here, Paul calls for genuine love that is unhypocritical. Greek scholar A. T. Robertson asserted, "Hypocritical or pretended love is no love at all."[1]

---

1   A. T. Robertson, *Word Pictures in the New Testament Vol. 4* (Nashville: Broadman Press, 1933), 62, Logos Bible Software.

Every expression of our faith should be offered with sincere and genuine care for the well-being of others.

One of the biggest misunderstandings among Christians is that we can have intimate fellowship with God but not be in fellowship with other believers. We can commune with God but merely tolerate our brothers and sisters. We can love God and hate our neighbor. However, such thinking falls apart when we look at Scripture. The apostle John wrote, "If someone says, 'I love God,' and hates his brother, he is a liar; for the one who does not love his brother whom he has seen, cannot love God whom he has not seen" (1 John 4:20).

Paul pivots in Romans 12:9 from love and calls believers to "abhor what is evil." We are to hate what is wrong, evil, and wicked. Where there is love, evil is not only to be grieved, but also to be hated. This simple command rescues us from many false ideas of what love is, lest we think that love means being a doormat that never contends for or opposes anything. Any love that is marked by indifference and neglect is not a true expression of love. It's a sham. As we present ourselves to God, we will find that our attitudes, feelings, and actions about love start to change, as the Holy Spirit renews our minds. We begin to embrace a new standard for living that brings glory to our Redeemer and joy to our hearts.

These commands to love and hate take me to the cross of Christ where I find their ultimate expression. At the cross, "Steadfast love and faithfulness meet; righteousness and peace kiss each other" (Psa. 85:10). At the cross, the mercy of God flows to sinners in love, and the wrath of God is poured out upon Jesus as a once-for-all payment for our guilt and a timeless statement of God's hatred for sin.

Brotherly and Sisterly Affection

In Romans 12:10, Paul exhorts believers to "love one another with brotherly affection." This calls for the type of loyalty and care that family members should have for one another. When believers love this way, they allow for weaknesses and imperfections.

This is a counter-cultural commitment. We have all mourned the erosion of family bonds in our culture. For example, one of the collateral concerns of the COVID-19 pandemic has been the welfare of children who cannot attend school. Change of routine, break in the learning process, missing significant life events, and loss of security and safety are major stresses on their lives.[2] Add to this trauma the widespread concern of increased child abuse because of more time at home. There is little comfort that the present state of the family will offer the support needed.

This is an opportunity for the church to offer loving support and be an example of a "family of families." We have a simple command given which should govern Body Life. We are to "love one another with brotherly affection" (v. 10). Paul modeled such a life in his relationships. In Romans 16, we find a list of names that is far more than just a list. Rather, it is a record of ministry partners in which Paul's love and commitment is showcased. Paul closes this letter by asking the church at Rome to greet these beloved brothers and sisters.

---

2   Centers for Disease Control and Prevention, "COVID-19 Parental Resources Kit-Childhood," accessed August 23, 2021, https://www.cdc.gov/coronavirus/2019-ncov/daily-life-coping/parental-resource-kit/childhood.html.

After commending Phoebe for her exemplary service in the church at Cenchreae, Paul refers to over twenty beloved ministry partners (Rom. 16:1–16). He refers to them in such a way that we are left with the strong impression that he would not have survived without their personal love and care. He says as much when he refers to Prisca and Aquila, "Who risked their necks for [his] life" (v. 4).

As we review this list in Romans 16, read between the lines with me. Listen to Paul's brotherly affection as he remembers these choice saints. Paul begins by greeting Epaenetus who was his first convert to Christ in Asia (v. 5); Mary, a woman who worked hard for the needs of the believers in Rome (v. 6); and fellow prisoners, Andronicus and Junia, who shared a special bond in the discomfort of jail (v. 7). Next, Paul refers to Ampliatus and Stachys, as being beloved in the Lord (vv. 8–9). He mentions Tryphaena and Tryphosa whom many scholars believe were twins and who made deposits into Paul's life (v. 12). Concerning Rufus, Paul refers to him as "chosen in the Lord," and with great tenderness, he refers to Rufus' mother as having "been a mother to me as well" (v. 13). In verse 14 includes a band of brothers—Asyncritus, Phlegon, Hermes, Patrobas, Hermas, as well as "the brothers who are with them." Paul closes by saying, "Greet one another with a holy kiss" (v. 16). What an amazing group of people! What a compelling example of family affection!

Relationships like these don't happen accidentally. This brings us back to Life on the Altar where the power of Christ within us to love like this is formed. We are called to pursue relationships in the church that are marked by love, truth, and perseverance. Following Paul's example in fostering relationships like these is needed now more than ever. We live in a culture that is spiraling out-of-control and at a time when the church is painfully divided. So, how do we as the church live differently than the world? How do we love as Paul loved and, more importantly, as Christ loved?

A Mess Worth Having

We tend to recoil and retreat when relationships sour. In their book, Timothy S. Lane and Paul David Tripp probe the question many ask—Why bother with relationships at all considering how they are often painful and troubling? They argue strongly, and biblically, that instead of calling for a détente on all relationships, we should see them from this perspective:

> God wants to bring us to the end of ourselves so that we would see our need for a relationship with him as well as with others. Every painful thing we experience in relationships is meant to remind us of our need for him. And every good thing we experience is meant to be a metaphor of what we can only find in him.[3]

Not only do we have to deal regularly with our own sinful attitudes and tendencies, which makes life hard enough, but we must work through painful relationships in the course of living as followers of Christ. God's plan is not to avoid problems but to work through them by His grace and for His glory. The

---

3   Timothy S. Lane and Paul David Tripp, *Relationships: A Mess Worthy Making* (Greensboro: New Growth Press, 2008), 7, Kindle edition.

relationships in a local church become the training ground for all believers to learn to love as Christ loves us (Eph. 4:31, 32). We are prone to speak in generalities about loving others. We prefer to love people from afar where they can't mess up our comforts and preferences. Truth be known, the adage describes us well, "To dwell above with the saints we love, Oh that will be glory; But to dwell below with the saints we know; Well, that's another story!"

We know such thinking will never do for the follower of Christ. God's plan is for us to live life together which allows us to give and receive in important ways. For a believer to move from one burned-out relationship to another communicates tremendous concern about their spiritual walk. Yet, I recognize that there are times to part when conscience and conviction collide. Indeed, some things are so messy that we must conclude that the conflict, as much as we would like to be reconciled, will have to be worked out at the judgment seat of Christ. Even so, let this be a call to each of us that as much as it depends upon us, we will pursue truth, peace, and love in our relationships (Rom. 12:18). This pursuit is empowered by thinking deeply about the commands of Romans 12 and living Life on the Altar.

Authentic relationships become one of the most compelling witnesses a church can exhibit. In our last chapter, we saw the early church in Acts 2 sacrificially care for each other. When a church loves in this way, it possesses a tremendous drawing power. Not only does it trumpet the gospel to needy hearts, but it sends forth God's truth to the next generation.

Multi-Generational Faithfulness in the Family of God

As I write this chapter, Gail Richardson, a member of our church, and his wife, Patsy, are the oldest living married couple in the state of Louisiana according to Louisiana Family Forum.[4] Our oldest member, Mae Hughes, is 104 at the time of this writing. In thinking of the makeup of our church family, we have five generations when we gather.

Baby dedications are a highlight for our church family. These dedications are really commitments of the parents to bring their child up in the nurture and admonition of the Lord (Deut. 6:1–18; Eph. 6:4). As parents stand before the church family with their child, this special moment acknowledges their prayers and commitments, and is a time for the church to express support. This support can be seen in how we nurture children growing up in the church family. What message do we want them to take away from having grown up in our church body? What memories will they have? My prayer is that God would leave an indelible impression on their hearts of the truth of Christ expressed with family affection.

Scripture calls God's people to multi-generational faithfulness. The psalmist expressed this beautifully, "One generation shall praise Your works to another and shall declare Your mighty acts" (Psa. 145:4 NASB). I find it interesting that the multi-generational relay of truth mentioned in this psalm is within the

---

4   Louisiana Family Forum, "Gail & Patsy Richardson-Married September 1, 1940," accessed September 2, 2021, https://lafamilyforum.org/2021longestmarriedfound/.

context of praise and worship. We are not merely to impart truth, coldly and dispassionately. A thousand times, "No!" We are to speak of the things of God in heartfelt praise and devotion. In other words, we are to commend the Lord and His saving work from hearts overflowing with love for God and for one another.

World Magazine shared the story of Ernesta Wood several years ago which captures the beauty of multi-generational faithfulness. Wood, who at the time of the article was 88 years old, displayed "photos of her 53 descendants, nearly all Christians. Once a week for the past 16 years, she has sent them letters—777 in all … filled with stories."[55] Some of her accounts are dramatic:

> Her blind grandmother miraculously saw Wood's grandfather minutes before he died. Other stories cultivate a sense of God's presence in less dramatic moments.…
>
> The letters testify about tragedies as well. Wood's first husband, Clyde, was a pastor and a pilot in training. He died in a plane crash when he was 54. Wood remembers sending her children to school that morning and praying, "Lord, help us to accept whatever happens to us today as from your hands." Then came a phone call: The plane was down, and one of the pilot's legs had burned. She assumed the other pilot (her husband) was hurt and drove to the hospital to pick him up. However, upon arrival, she learned he was dead. Wood stayed calm and wrote about the comfort of knowing her early morning prayer had been answered amid the family tragedy.

---

5   Kathryn Lewis, "Telling the Works," *World Magazine*, accessed August 1, 2021, https://world.wng.org/2019/08/telling_the_works.

After her husband's death, Wood moved in with her parents, then traveled as a teacher with the Jesus Film Project. She lived in Russia for a year and wrote to her grandchildren that the exact amount of money needed for her to live overseas that year, $27,000, miraculously came the day it was due. She wrote about new converts, prayers answered, and joy. Wood also visited Mongolia, Cambodia, South Africa, Croatia, and other countries. She hated flying, especially after her husband's death, but she embraced the adventures and chronicled stories of God's worldwide work.

In 2007, Wood, then 76, married Cliff Wood, 80, five months after their first date. More than 700 guests attended their wedding, and two grandsons served as the officiating pastors. While giving a tour of the grandchildren's photos hanging on the walls, Wood laughs at a photo of her and Cliff, two octogenarians, rolling by the White House on Segways. She remembers blowing past another elderly lady in a wheelchair who shouted, "You go, girl!" That could be Wood's refrain, as each of her weekly letters quotes Psalm 118:17: "I will not die, but live, and tell of the works of the Lord."[6]

What a great example of multi-generational faithfulness!

Commitments around the New Covenant

A major step of growth for our church family was the recovery of covenant church membership. What does that mean? In

---

6   Ibid.

simple terms, we have sought to reclaim that church membership matters. Our church bond is a covenant relationship under
the new covenant established by Jesus Christ. Some churches
have in their tradition a covenantal statement that outlines biblical commitments the congregation agrees to pursue under
the Lordship of Christ. In 2006, we blew the dust off our own
church covenant and performed an extensive reworking of the
document. With great care not to add to the gospel, our church
covenant expresses biblical goals and commitments, including
church membership, that flow from the text of Scripture and the
grace found in Christ. Consider the following from our church
covenant that pertains to family affection. We commit:

> To walk together in Christian love; to seek the
> salvation of our family, friends, and acquaintances;
> to avoid such conduct as gossip, unkind words
> and excessive anger; to watch over one another in
> brotherly love, to remember one another in prayer,
> to aid one another in sickness and distress; to
> cultivate Christian sympathy in feeling and Christian
> courtesy in speech; to be slow to take offense, but
> always ready for reconciliation and mindful of the
> rules of our Savior to secure it without delay.[7]

Life on the Altar should lead to a life of familial affection
toward other believers, especially in the local church. This commitment among believers is to be strong and loyal. The family
affection called for in Scripture is not based on human sentiment but is anchored in the redeeming love of Jesus Christ. A

---

7   First Baptist Church Gonzales, Louisiana, "Church Covenant," accessed August
    21, 2021, https://www.fbcg.net/covenant.

church covenant is a helpful tool to remind us of our commitments to the Scriptures and to each other. Christ is the source of all forgiveness and reconciliation. This kind of bond will hold any church together, no matter what threats may come from outside or inside the body.

Ever the Best of Friends

There is a scene in Charles Dickens' classic, *Great Expectations*, that demonstrates committed love. The main character, Pip, is a young boy who, upon the death of his parents, was placed in the care of his sister and her husband, a man named Joe Gargery. The sister was a mean-spirited woman who exploited Pip for financial gain. Joe, however, was a Christ-like man, humble, hardworking, and kind.

Through a mysterious benefactor, Pip was given a fortune when he came of age. When the time came, Pip left the poverty of the forge and made his way to London to pursue a gentleman's life in Victorian England.

Leaving the humble setting of the forge, Pip soon forgot the kindnesses of Joe, his adoptive father. Pip became embarrassed by his unprivileged past and even by the appearance of Joe who came to visit him in London. Pip's life began to unravel as he took on debt and made one unwise decision after another. In time, Pip found himself in legal trouble and his fortune depleted. In one of the greatest scenes from Dickens' work, Joe learned of Pip's plight and paid the fee for his release. It was all that Joe had, and he made no demands for repayment.

In humility and brokenness, Pip returned to the home of his upbringing. When he arrived, Pip offered a sincere apology, realizing that he had depleted Joe's resources for his release. Joe's response is stunning as he says to this young man who had been under his care for most of his childhood, "'O dear old Pip, old chap,' said Joe. 'God knows as I forgive you, if I have anything to forgive!'"[8] Joe's continual refrain to his wayward nephew was that they were "ever the best of friends."[9]

The need for brotherly affection comes at a time when the bonds of fellowship are frayed in both family and church. This is not a new development. We read of conflict in the New Testament that truly stretched the relationships, and some were severed. This command is a reminder to us all when the rhetoric and hostility are at a feverish pitch. May we seek to contend earnestly for the faith with love and respect toward one another.

Altar Moments

1. What are some of the challenges you face in expressing family affection in church life? Read Ephesians 4:29–32. How would the instruction of these verses help you in those relationships?

2. What are ways that you can promote multi-generational faithfulness in your church? Read Deuteronomy 6:1–18. How should this text challenge our efforts to disciple younger generations?

---

8 Charles Dickens, *Great Expectations*, public domain, location 7094, Kindle edition.
9 Ibid, location 6931.

3. Jesus spoke of the new covenant when He instituted the Lord's Supper (Matt. 26:28). How should we live under this new covenant? How do passages like Romans 12 motivate godly living?

4. Paul and Barnabas had a blowup in their relationship. Read Acts 15:36–41. What was the problem? Was that the end of the story? Consider Colossians 4:10 and 2 Timothy 4:11. How did the disagreement end?

Prayer:

Dear Lord Jesus Christ,

I realize that no one loves the church more than You do. You have purchased us from every tribe and land with Your blood and righteousness. For my part in Your kingdom work, may I be a peacemaker, as well as a truth-speaker. Help me to promote unity in the body of Christ based upon the truth of Your Word. Keep me from contributing harm to the church's witness through careless words, reckless actions, or selfish pursuits. When issues of conscience and conviction demand that I stand, or even depart, may I do so with grace and wisdom. Revive Your church, O Lord, and may we be salt and light for this generation. May we live out the gospel with one another and may it receive a fresh hearing in our day.

For the Glory of Your Name, Amen.

Chapter 8

Living the
"One Another's"

"And let us consider how to stir up one another to
love and good works." Hebrews 10:24

IN 2007, FBCG PREPARED for its centennial celebration.
While doing so, I discovered that our church was formed
around the same time as some large, well-known companies,
including Harley Davidson, United Parcel Service (UPS), Blue
Bell, Walgreens, and Kellogg's. In thinking about our church of a
few hundred compared to these corporate giants, I was taken by
both the contrast in size and purpose between us. These companies have massive resources for the communication and sale of
their products, while our little congregation operates on a com-
paratively meager budget.

It was a reminder for me that God's work is done in this world
not by a show of might, nor by political power but through the
empowerment of the Holy Spirit. The church is charged with

LIFE ON THE ALTAR

declaring and living the message of grace found in Jesus Christ, and we trace our roots to the gospel movement recorded in the New Testament over two thousand years ago. Jesus' parting words to the disciples were to go into all the world and proclaim this good news (Matt. 28:19). Every church is given that honor, and this mission is given with God's promised success.

Christ Will Build His Church

Jesus asked His disciples at Caesarea Philippi, "Who do people say that the Son of Man is?" (Matt. 16:13). Peter answered, "You are the Christ, the Son of the living God" (v. 16). Jesus commended Peter saying, "Blessed are you, Simon Bar-Jonah! For flesh and blood has not revealed this to you, but my Father who is in heaven. And I tell you, you are Peter, and on this rock I will build my church, and the gates of hell shall not prevail against it" (vv. 17–18). Jesus promised to build His church, and that it would be indestructible.

How does Christ build His church? One of the great success stories of history is how a humble band of believers were sent out from Jerusalem to spread the message of their Savior. We are reminded of that every time believers gather. Collectively, we could say that we are meeting today in Jesus' name because the first disciples were faithful to their charge.

Every generation of believers is called to follow the same pattern of ministry. Christ builds His church through the spread of the gospel. Believers are called to make disciples and plant local churches. The redemptive work of Christ is meant to be displayed before neighborhoods, as well as the nations. There is not an improved plan in the making. There is no "Plan B" in the works concerning the Great Commission. Jesus' last command to the disciples was to engage in this mission until the end of the age (Matt. 28:19–20).

The church is called to be "the pillar and support of the truth" (1 Tim. 3:15). Every local body should live for the purpose that God would be glorified "in the church and in Christ Jesus throughout all generations" (Eph. 3:21). The language of the New Testament references the church, both universal and local, as the base of God's kingdom purposes in this world and God's plan for the ages (Eph. 3:1–13).

Unfortunately, many do not share this understanding of the church. A local church is often portrayed as a lethargic, pathetic gathering which is relegated in the minds of some as a place where you might get married or buried. It's a place for old people to gather, and they do so out of a duty-bound allegiance to keep the institution going. In the mind of detractors, the church is seen as a relic of the past; while they should be allowed to exist, they should do so quietly. Others see the church more cynically as a drain on resources, as an institution that should die a natural death. Thoughts of church life impacting one's soul, changing one's life, or carrying any sort of value is not seen by the critics. Even among those who identify with a church, the grand and glorious picture found in the New Testament often seems far removed.

This is what makes Jesus' conversation with Peter in Matthew 16 monumental in our understanding of the church's future. Christ pledges to build His church, and nothing can stop this sovereign movement of God. Os Guinness expressed in an interview, "Jesus made clear that the kingdom of God is organic and not organizational. It grows like a seed and it works like leaven: secretly, invisibly, surprisingly, and irresistibly."[1] As history steps forward, it does so with purpose, as all things will be brought in submission to Christ (Eph. 1:22–23). God is gathering a people for His name. The way this redemption comes and the way Christ builds His church is through the proclamation of the gospel.

The Church and Ultimate Issues

Our centennial celebration brought about a renewed love for Christ's church. My prayer was that we would reflect Christ's love for one another and demonstrate that through meaningful ministry. I was reminded in my comparison with corporate giants mentioned previously that the church is the only institution called into existence to deal with the ultimate issues: life and death, forgiveness, reconciliation, marriage, purpose for living, and true community.

I thought of how interaction with these companies is much different than a fellowship connection with a local church. For example, you wouldn't walk into a Harley Davidson dealership and say to the salesman, "I've got cancer and the doctor says that I only have a few months to live. How should I process this news? Would you have a customer service specialist who could

---

1   Ginny Mooney, "Os Guinness Calls for a New Christian Renaissance," *The Christian Post*, accessed March 10, 2021, https://www.christianpost.com/news/os-guinness-calls-for-a-new-christian-renaissance.html.

meet with me to talk about my future? Would you have the company pray for me?"

You wouldn't go to the Walgreens Pharmacy and ask, "Do you have any medicine that will give meaning for my life and hope beyond the casket? The Scripture tells all of us that we have an appointment with death, and then the judgment (Heb. 9:27). I was wondering if you had something that would bring peace to my soul and reconciliation with a holy God as I face these realities?"

We could imagine similar responses to major life events from other companies such as Blue Bell, Kellogg's, and UPS. I'm not speaking disparagingly of these companies, but their purpose is to sell motorcycles or to provide prescriptions. They do not exist to point to eternal realities. However, this is precisely what the church is commissioned to do by Christ himself. If you want to be a part of God's saving enterprise in this world, immersion in a local, gospel-centered church is the place to be.[2]

The Church Is Meant to Be an Oasis of Grace

God's redeemed people are those who gather under the banner of His grace and are committed to serve one another. The church was birthed to minister grace to human brokenness

---

2   My reference to a gospel-centered church is the picture given in the New Testament which outlines the following commitments: right preaching of the gospel (Gal. 1:6–9); observance of the ordinances of baptism and Lord's Supper (Matt. 28:19; 26:26–29); accountability to one another through church discipline (Matt. 18:15–20; 1 Cor. 5:1–12); and biblical leadership (1 Tim. 3:1–13; Titus 1:6–9). These commitments should be considered thoughtfully and prayerfully before uniting with a local body.

through proclaiming the gospel. Every local body exists to be an oasis of grace.

Is this true of your church? Is it a gathering where love is expressed and sacrificial ministry is modeled? One way we can be used to transform stale church life is a renewed focus of practicing the "one another" verses in Scripture. By this, I'm referring to over thirty commands found in the New Testament that call believers to minister to one another. Let's take a look at these simple commands. May they serve as a lamp unto our feet and a light unto our path regarding Body Life.

Practicing the "One Another" Commands

A local church becomes an oasis of grace, as we learn to give of ourselves and to receive from others. Take a moment and reflect on the "one another" commands below:

- Love one another (John 13:34–35)
- Bear one another's burdens (Gal. 6:2)
- Depend upon one another (Rom. 12:5)
- Be kind to one another (Eph. 4:32)
- Be devoted to one another (Rom.12:10)
- Forgive one another (Eph. 4:32)
- Honor one another (Rom. 12:10)
- Submit to one another (Eph. 5:21)
- Rejoice with one another (Rom. 12:15)
- Uphold one another (Eph. 4:2; Col. 3:13)
- Weep with one another (Rom. 12:15)
- Same mind (Rom. 12:16)
- Encourage one another (1 Thess. 5:11)
- Be tenderhearted to one another (Eph. 4:32)
- Do not judge one another (Rom 14:13)

- Stimulate one another (Heb. 10:24)
- Accept one another (Rom. 15:7)
- Don't speak evil of one another (Jas. 4:11)
- Admonish one another (Rom. 15:14)
- Not grumble against one another (Jas. 5:9)
- Salute one another (Rom. 16:16)
- Confess our faults to one another (Jas. 5:16)
- Fellowship with one another (1 John 1:7)
- Pray for one another (Jas 5:16)
- Wait for one another (I Cor. 11:33)
- Show hospitality to one another (1 Pet. 4:9)
- Care for one another (I Cor. 12:25)
- Minister gifts to one another (1 Pet. 4:10)
- Serve one another (Gal. 5:13)
- Don't be prideful toward one another (1 Cor. 4:6)
- Humble ourselves toward one another (1 Pet. 5:5)

These are simple but life-changing commands. They give direction on how to live for Christ. They call for action and for the exercising of our faith. Interestingly, one-third of these "one another" commands are found in Romans 12–16. We are members of one another in the same spiritual body (12:5). We have a shared union with Christ and should cultivate attitudes of support and love toward others. We are to be devoted to one another and honor one another (12:10). Our relationships are to be marked by care and respect. We are to share the full continuum of life from rejoicing to weeping with one another (12:15). We are to seek unity and the same mind as we serve the Lord (12:16). We are not to judge one another harshly as we exercise our liberty in Christ (14:13). We are to receive one another with acceptance (15:7), as well as admonish one another when concerns and dangers arise (15:14). Closing out the "one another's" in Romans, we are to salute, greet, embrace one another as an appropriate expression of our love for one another (16:16). Life on the Altar is given to obeying these "one another" commands.

It's well-established that Christians aren't perfect people. I doubt you need much convincing that this is true. But I would say that while Christians still sin, they are fundamentally different people because of the call placed upon their lives. They've been enabled by the grace of the Lord Jesus Christ to show that love in how they love one another. Such a commitment in a believer's life pushes us forward in Christian service. These commands get us off the sidelines and onto the field of ministry. They rescue Christians from a deadly consumer mentality that breeds selfishness. A pursuit of the "one another" commands points us to a Christlike life. This is ministry every believer can embrace; indeed, every believer is commanded to embrace. Together, we as Christians should pursue making our local church, whether small or large, the oasis of grace it was meant to be.

Think of the impact fulfilling these "one another" commitments would bring to a church, to a city, to a nation, and to this groaning world. No wonder Aristides, the erudite Athenian philosopher, offered this defense of Christianity to the Roman Emperor Hadrian:

> Falsehood is not found among them; and they love one another, and from widows they do not turn away their esteem; and they deliver the orphan from him who treats him harshly. And he, who has, gives to him who has not, without boasting. And when they

see a stranger, they take him in to their homes and rejoice over him as a very brother; for they do not call them brethren after the flesh, but brethren after the spirit and in God. And whenever one of their poor passes from the world, each one of them according to his ability gives heed to him and carefully sees to his burial. And if they hear that one of their number is imprisoned or afflicted on account of the name of their Messiah, all of them anxiously minister to his necessity, and if it is possible to redeem him they set him free. And if there is among them any that is poor and needy, and if they have no spare food, they fast two or three days in order to supply to the needy their lack of food.[3]

That is quite a challenge, isn't it? God intends for His people to be a visual model of the gospel. He wants us to live our lives together in such a way that we demonstrate the good news of reconciliation before a fractured world.

How Big of a Deal Is It for You to Miss Church?

With over thirty "one another" commands in the New Testament, which are intended to be put into practice by God's people, some questions claw in my mind. Is neglect of your local church a sin? Is it sinful for a believer to forsake the gathering of their local church?

---

3   Aristides of Athens, A. Menzies ed., D. M. Kay trans., *The Apology of Aristides Volume 9* (New York: Christian Literature Company, 1897), 277, Logos Bible Software.

Simply put, if you have the flu, please stay home. If you are away on a vacation, enjoy yourself! If you are called to intensive work assignments, to a military deployment, or to pursue a college education, or any other endeavor that would call you away, please fulfill those responsibilities while your church prays for you in such times. But I don't think illness or the other things mentioned are the reason that absenteeism is so widespread.

Yes, there are times when "the ox is in the ditch" and absence from the body is necessary. However, there appear to be a lot of oxen in trouble to justify the abandonment of church life presently seen. Widespread absenteeism occurs because of the sin of forsaking the church. The writer of Hebrews spoke of this sin of neglecting the gathering of believers (Heb. 10:25). He even noted that some were doing this as a habit. A. T. Robertson commented on the danger of forsaking the gathering of the church, when he said, "Already some Christians had formed the habit of not attending public worship, a perilous habit then and now."[4] The sin of forsaking your church could be understood as deliberately absenting yourself from the church body as a habit of life. It is sad to me what people are willing to substitute for gathering with their church. Trivial things, temporal matters, often carry the priority of time and resources in the lives of professing Christians. This misplacement of priorities does not reconcile with Jesus' command to seek first the kingdom of God (Matt. 6:33).

At the heart of church life should be a covenant commitment that binds us together in common fellowship and purpose. Our

---

4   A. T. Robertson, *Word Pictures in the New Testament, Vol. 5* (Nashville: Broadman Press, 1933), 82–83, Logos Bible Software.

biblical identity is not a loose band of believers doing whatever they want. Rather, we observe in the New Testament the church brought together under the tight cords of the new covenant. We have not been well-taught on what it means to be a people gathered into a local church by covenant, which has been the understanding of Christians in the past for their public witness as a disciple of Jesus Christ. The absence of a conviction regarding covenant membership comes easily in our culture of individualism.

We must return to the truth that God has always called His people to come together regularly and consistently. We are given no indication that God ever intended for believers to survive on their own without the fellowship, nurture, instruction, and encouragement of a local church.

The Old Testament illustrates this truth in stunning language. The Day of Atonement carried with it a stiff judgment as God said, "For any person who does any work on this same day, that person I will destroy" (Lev. 23:27). The judgment for the one who neglected the Passover was equally sobering for such a "person was to be cut off from his people, for he did not present the offering of the Lord at its appointed time" (Num. 9:13). In the milieu of ancient Israel, can you imagine an Israelite ever thinking, "You know, I'm not into the feasts. I can serve God just as well in my own way. I don't need the priests or the tabernacle. I don't need to offer the sacrifices." Such neglect and arrogance would have been deadly, quite literally.

I'm not arguing as a legalist, but I do want us to see the intensity of the Old Testament admonitions regarding the sanctity of

Israel's worship. Neglecting the gathering of the people of God was not an option for those under the old covenant nor is it for those under the new covenant.

This biblical fervor and understanding have been present in church history. For example, Greg Wills noted in his work *Democratic Religion* that during the Civil War, Southern Baptists removed an average of 2% of their membership annually. At the same time, their churches demonstrated rapid growth.[5] Mark Dever researched the minutes of church meetings in the 1800's and discovered that nonattendance was "considered one of the most sinister of sins, because it usually veiled other sins. When someone began to be in sin, they would usually stop attending."[6] This expressed conviction indicated an attitude about the church in which the ongoing, willful neglect of the gathering was one of the worst transgressions one could commit because it served as a cloak for every other sin.

While believers may be sluggish to embrace commitment to their local church, our culture understands the sin of forsaking. On one Rotary International website, I read this statement: "Rotarians count on one another to contribute their time to weekly meetings, committee work, and service events. 100% attendance is urged and honored in Rotary. Try not only to attend all the meetings, but also to stay for the full program and give

5   Gregory A. Wills, *Democratic Religion: Freedom, Authority, and Church Discipline in the Baptist South, 1785–1900* (New York: Oxford University Press, 1996) 22, quoted in Mark Dever, *Nine Marks of a Healthy Church, 3rd edition* (Wheaton: Crossway, 2013), location 1715, Kindle edition.
6   Ibid, location 2806.

each speaker your complete attention."[7] Another Rotary website expressed the consequences clearly, "If the member fails to attend as required, the member's membership shall be subject to termination."[8] These local clubs understand forsaking and neglecting one's membership.

Team sports understand too. If you say to your son's coach, "Coach, we don't like practice and don't really want to be identified with the team in that way. Just keep us on the roster (and the starting line-up!), and we will show up when we can work it in." We all know such a response would be unacceptable. You can't keep a team on the field with that type of commitment.

The academic world also understands the sin of forsaking. A college student I know was touching base with her professor before an upcoming mission trip. She expressed to him why she would miss class in the coming week. He said bluntly, "I don't care if you are hung over or on a mission trip, you have two absences for the semester, that's it." Why would he be so demanding? Well, because education is a serious commitment that is lost with poor attendance.

So, what would never be acceptable in a civic club or in athletics or in education is freely accepted when it comes to the things of Christ and His Church. I believe this neglect is much of the reason why the Church in North America has little power and a blemished witness.

---

7   Rotary Club of Saratoga Springs, New York, "Become a Member," accessed August 31, 2021, https://www.saratogaspringsrotary.org/SitePage/ membership-information.

8   Rotary Club of Wheaton, Illinois, "Bylaws," accessed September 1, 2021, https:// clubrunner.blob.core.windows.net/00000002412/en-ca/files/homepage/by-laws-2018/Wheaton-Rotary-ByLaws-2018.pdf.

Commitment to our local church is critical for the health of our soul and has a ripple effect to future generations. Our faithfulness to the gospel is dependent upon the life we live in a local body. It has been said that the church seldom resurrects what the home puts to death. It is unlikely that future generations will embrace the value of church life if parents treat church attendance with flimsy efforts. Fellow sojourner, schedule your life around the gathering of your local church. Prepare your heart to gather with your church family. Review and seek to apply the "one another's" as you come together. Your union with Christ bonds you to your Savior and to fellow believers. Don't forsake what God has established to bring you untold blessings.

Altar Moments

1. Do you agree that the church of Jesus Christ exists to give answers to ultimate issues? Read Ephesians 3:1–13. What insight do these verses give to the church's role in God's purposes?

2. Read Matthew 16:13–20. How does Christ build His church? Does it strengthen your faith and resolve when you read that Christ will build His church and the gates of hell will not prevail against it? What does that mean when all is said and done?

3. How do you prepare to attend your church? Do you go with a focus on practicing the "one another" commands? Consider praying through the list of the "one another's" in the New

Testament and use them to prepare for your gathering with your church family.

Prayer:

> Dear Lord of the Church,
>
> Help me to love what You love. Nothing is clearer from reading the New Testament than Your love for the church. Renew my mind regarding my attitudes concerning Body Life. Refresh my love for fellow believers, as we share the common bond of being in Christ. Help me to put off every excuse that keeps me from giving my best to Your kingdom causes. Help me to see that You have placed me in a spiritual family for Your glory, for the building up of Your church, and for my spiritual growth. May I serve You faithfully through my local church, and as we gather this week, give me eyes to see ways that I can minister the "one another's." May I sense Your pleasure, as I walk in obedience unto You.
>
> In Your Majestic and Holy Name, Amen.

Chapter 9

Gifts Needed
for the Journey

"To each is given the manifestation of the Spirit
for the common good." 1 Corinthians 12:7

SOME OF THE MOST comforting promises in the New Testament are those that refer to the Holy Spirit's ministry in the life of the believer. My thoughts immediately go to the Upper Room and Jesus' parting words to the disciples. After the shock and awe of His announced departure, Jesus said to them, "And I will ask the Father, and he will give you another Helper, to be with you forever, even the Spirit of truth, whom the world cannot receive, because it neither sees him nor knows him. You know him, for he dwells with you and will be in you" (John 14:16–17). Jesus pledged that He would not leave His disciples as orphans. With His departure "another Helper" would come who would be like Him in supplying everything needed to obey His commission. As we can imagine, this was a difficult teaching for the twelve disciples to understand. How would this happen?

Pentecost came and the Spirit of the living God was given to the church (Acts 2:1–47). The disciples began to understand that God did not dwell in a building made with hands (Acts 17:24), but the living God dwelt within every believer, just as Christ had promised. In Paul's letters, he would emphasize the seal of the Spirit on the believer's life (Eph. 1:13–14) and that "anyone who does not have the Spirit of Christ does not belong to him" (Rom. 8:9). Through the saving work of Christ, the new covenant established that God's law would not be written on tablets of stone but on the heart of every believer. The prophet Ezekiel referenced the new covenant with great hope, as he declared the Word of the Lord: "And I will give you a new heart, and a new spirit I will put within you. And I will remove the heart of stone from your flesh and give you a heart of flesh. And I will put my Spirit within you and cause you to walk in my statutes and be careful to obey my rules" (Ezek. 36:26–27). God has given these tremendous promises to His blood-bought people.

The Ongoing Work of the Holy Spirit

Many times, the New Testament presents the importance of the Holy Spirit's ministry in the life of the church. Beginning with regeneration, believers are baptized by the Spirit (1 Cor. 12:12–13).[1] We are commanded to walk by the Spirit in our pursuit of an obedient life before God (Gal. 5:16). Also, in Galatians 5, the fruit of the Spirit is presented by Paul as virtues that should be in the believer's life as opposed to the deeds of the flesh (vv. 17–23).

---

1   In John 3:3–8, Jesus referred to the regenerating work of the Spirit as being "born again."

Believers are called to be filled with the Holy Spirit. This command occurs in the present tense, which communicates a continual action of being carried along by the Spirit. In Ephesians 5:18, Paul uses the verb *pleróō*, meaning "to fill, to make full." The idea behind this command is to be continually filled with the Holy Spirit. Paul describes the Spirit-filled life as one marked by a deep fellowship with God, including a life of abundant joy, thanksgiving, and submission. Using similar language in Colossians 3:16, Paul urges believers to "let the word of Christ dwell in you richly," providing insight to what it means to be filled with the Holy Spirit. The Spirit's filling in the believer's life is allowing the Word of God to dwell within us in such a way that it brings the fruit of obedience in the moment-by-moment demands of life.

The Spirit's Power for Altar Living

The Holy Spirit's power is essential to presenting ourselves to God as living sacrifices. Life on the Altar is not empowered by human grit but by the Holy Spirit. We can include the beautiful ministry of the Spirit as one of the "mercies of God" mentioned by Paul in Romans 12:1.

There are twenty-seven references to the Holy Spirit in the letter of Romans. Chapter 8 carries the lion's share of these references. Paul writes of the active work of the Holy Spirit on behalf of the believer seventeen times. This chapter is a treasure trove of insight into the Spirit's work in the believer's life.[2]

---

2 Romans 8:4–6, 9–11, 13–16, 26–27.

These are amazing promises! Life in the Spirit is one of the most treasured blessings we can know, because the Holy Spirit supplies the power of God to our frail life and efforts. Through the indwelling Holy Spirit:

- We can live pleasing and obedient lives before the Lord.
- Our minds are continually renewed for God's purposes.
- We are empowered to overcome sin.
- We are led as sons of God.
- We are adopted into God's forever family, and He becomes our "Abba! Father!"
- We are helped by the Holy Spirit moment-by-moment because He intercedes for us.

The Holy Spirit's Help and Intercession

R. A. Torrey (1856–1928) was a man of scholarship, as well as devotion. He graduated from Yale Divinity School and studied in Germany. He pastored what would become Moody Church in Chicago and provided oversight of the Moody Bible Institute. Later, Torrey would be instrumental in founding Biola University in Los Angeles.

Torrey's faith was refined in the crucible of suffering. He explained in his booklet, *Death Defeated and Defied: A Message of Comfort, Consolation, and Cheer*, that "[a] little daughter aged nine years and twelve days, left our home to go to be with Christ."[3] This little girl, named Elizabeth, died from a childhood disease. The funeral came, and as they looked at the grave, Torrey's wife was heard saying, "I am so glad that Elizabeth is not in

---

3   R. A. Torrey, *Death Defeated and Defied: A Message of Comfort, Consolation, and Cheer* (Los Angeles: Biola Publications, 1923), 41–42.

that box!"[4] They made their way home, carrying their grief from the cemetery with them.

The next morning, though exhausted, Torrey began his walk on the streets of Chicago toward the Bible Institute to teach his classes. As he passed around the corner of Chestnut Street and LaSalle Avenue, he could not contain his grief any longer. The loss overtook him, causing him to pause and cry out, "Oh, Elizabeth! Elizabeth!"[5] His grief broke over him as he felt the loneliness of her absence, the terrible feeling that they would never hear her laughter again, never see her face, and never witness her growth. As he paused on the street, he began to pray, and this is what he experienced:

> And just then this fountain that I had in my heart broke forth with such power as I think I had never experienced before, and it was the most joyful moment that I had ever known in my life! Oh, how wonderful is the joy of the [Spirit]! It is an unspeakably glorious thing to have your joy, not in things without you, not even in your most dearly loved friends, but to have within you a fountain ever springing up, springing up, springing up, always springing up, three hundred and sixty-five days in every year, springing up under all circumstances into everlasting life.[6]

---

4   R. A. Torrey, *The Holy Spirit: Who He Is and What He Does And How to Know Him in All the Fullness of His Gracious and Glorious Ministry* (Greenville, SC: Ambassador Emerald International, 2006), 107.

5   Ibid.

6   Ibid.

Life on the Altar requires the Spirit's power and enablement. Living for Christ is not something we accomplish in our strength. Jesus told his disciples, "Apart from me, you can do nothing" (John 15:5). How wonderful that God has given to us the Holy Spirit, who accomplishes within us and through us works we could never do on our own!

The Spirit and the Gifts Are Ours

Martin Luther's famous hymn, "A Mighty Fortress Is Our God," reminds us of the church's need for the Holy Spirit's empowerment to advance Christ's kingdom. In the hymn, Luther describes the cosmic battle between the Prince of Darkness, who has no equal on this earth, and the Lord God Almighty who is sovereign. We are warned in verse two not to trust in our own abilities: "Did we in our own strength confide, Our striving would be losing."[7] Our efforts to advance in this spiritual struggle will be in vain if we rest in our own resources. The hymn concludes with great triumph and encouragement for the people of God. God's victory is sure because His Word is above all earthly powers. God will have the final say. Until then, believers are encouraged in the battle because "the Spirit and the gifts are ours through him who with us sideth."[8]

In addition to the different aspects of the Holy Spirit's ministry mentioned above, Paul spent considerable effort instructing the church on spiritual gifts. The New Testament provides five

---

7   Martin Luther, "A Mighty Fortress Is Our God," public domain.
8   Ibid.

instances in which spiritual gifts are listed.[9] The lists are varied, with nineteen gifts mentioned in all. Sometimes, different words are used to describe the same gift as with serving and helping. Romans 12:6–8 highlights one of these lists. The text reads,

> **Having gifts that differ according to the grace given
> to us, let us use them: if prophecy, in proportion
> to our faith; if service, in our serving; the one who
> teaches, in his teaching; the one who exhorts, in his
> exhortation; the one who contributes, in generosity;
> the one who leads, with zeal; the one who does acts of
> mercy, with cheerfulness.**

Paul wrote to challenge believers to use their spiritual gifts with urgency and purpose. Sadly, many are like the disciples in Acts 19 who responded to Paul's question about the Holy Spirit by saying, "We have not even heard that there is a Holy Spirit" (Acts 19:2). Their ignorance was honest, as they were experiencing the transition from the old covenant to the new covenant without the aid of the New Testament. They needed to be taught what God had done through Christ and through the subsequent miracle of Pentecost to empower them to live the Christian life. Twenty-one centuries removed, we are living at a time in God's redemptive history where "the Spirit and the gifts are ours."[10] Life on the Altar is lived in the power of the indwelling Holy Spirit as we use the gifts and talents God has given to us.

---

9   Rom. 12:6–8; 1 Cor. 12:8–10, 28–30; Eph. 4:11; and 1 Pet. 4:10–11. 1 Cor. 14 should also be considered as a chapter that speaks to the application of spiritual gifts in Body Life.

10 Luther, "A Mighty Fortress Is Our God," public domain.

The Christian life is meant to be an informed spirituality—God wants us to know how He has gifted us for His kingdom work. As we discussed in Chapter 5, we discern God's will for our lives in part by our desires (Rom. 12:2). In church life, the desire of a believer to do a particular ministry informs how God has gifted us spiritually. However, one's desire needs to be affirmed through the confirmation of others in the body. This protects against a believer thinking they are gifted in a certain way when they may not be. We are called to encourage one another in our service in Christ's kingdom. God's bestowal of spiritual gifts is a divine enablement for the task at hand. They are gifts for the journey, and we should use them for God's glory. In our look at Altar Life, several truths emerge from Romans 12 regarding spiritual gifts.

God Has Given a Great Diversity of Gifts in the Body

In Romans 12, we look once more to Paul's emphasis on the unity and diversity of the body of Christ: "For as in one body we have many members, and the members do not all have the same function, so we, though many, are one body in Christ, and individually members one of another" (vv. 4–5). God's plan for His church is for the many members to be equipped for ministry to showcase His grace before the world.

First, we must understand that every believer has a spiritual gift. Romans 12:3–8 implies that each Christian has at least one gift. There should never be a diminishing of the value of a believer's spiritual gift among the people of God. Scripture affirms that no believer is unnecessary (1 Cor. 12:14–20). One of the important pursuits in the Christian life is to identify how God has gifted us to meet temporal needs, as well as to make an eternal impact. Asking helpful questions within a church family can help members identify their spiritual gifts. As ministry opportunities arise and are promoted in church life, members should ask, "What do I have a desire to do? What do I have a passion to do? Do I have joy when I serve in this way?" Answering these basic questions can aid a believer in discovering their spiritual gift(s). Seeking to understand how we are gifted is not meant to be mechanical, and it should never be an excuse for disobeying God's Word.

Secondly, there should be an urgency to serve. In Romans 12:7–8, Paul underscores how we are to use our spiritual gifts. He comments particularly on the spiritual gifts of giving with generosity, leading with zeal, and giving mercy with cheerfulness. Commentators have discussed why Paul would stress the way these gifts should be exercised. Perhaps the strongest reason for Paul's emphasis is that these gifts can suffer from lethargy and half-hearted efforts.

For those who have the gift of giving, the charge is to give sacrificially. Give for maximum impact for the cause of Christ! Give magnanimously for the needs of others!

For those who have leadership gifts, Paul urges to lead with zeal. This is a call for leaders, for the Lord's sake, to lead! Schreiner identified one of the dangers of leadership when he said, "Leaders are more prone to laziness than others simply because there may be no one exercising oversight of them. Thus, they may be able to skate by with less than a zealous effort."[11] Leaders seem to find alcoves in which to hide when they fail to lead. Someone once remarked to me, "I had a pastor who had retired, but he just didn't know it." I suspect that he did know it, and the work suffered because of it. Those with gifts of leadership should lead with zeal because much is at stake.

Mercy is best expressed through the ministry of giving of oneself to others. This is front line ministry that can become consuming. Paul reminds those who may be weary from exercising the gift of mercy to continue doing so with cheerfulness for the glory of Christ.

Whether you are tempted to hold back or hide out or grumble about ministry, Paul's admonishments are timely and helpful. Whatever gift or gifts God has given to you, take your place among the people of God and give it all you've got! May we press forward with confidence and courage in the Spirit's power as we point our generation to the unsearchable riches of Jesus Christ.

Altar Moments

1. Have you thought about how God has gifted you spiritually? Give a look at the following passages and identify ways God has gifted you: Romans 12:6–8; 1 Corinthians 12:8–10, 28–30; Ephesians 4:11; and 1 Peter 4:10–11. What ministry do you desire to fulfill in the body of Christ? Seek ways to serve in your church's ministries. Identify service that brings you joy.

---

11 Schreiner, *Romans*, 660.

2. From the passages mentioned in this chapter from Romans 8, how does the ministry of the Holy Spirit encourage you? Help you? Empower you? Comfort you?

3. Have you grown weary in your service? Have you experienced setbacks and discouragement? May this challenge from Romans 12:3–8 inspire you to return to ministry.

Prayer:

"Triune God of all creation,

In the name of Jesus and for His glory,

Send your Holy Spirit to fashion this prayer for Christ's praise.

Where my heart lacks seriousness or sincerity, supply the Spirit's fervor.

Where my hands lack ability or direction, provide the Spirit's power and design.

Where my will lacks resolve or righteousness, let the Spirit convict, transform, and overrule.

By the Spirit, flood my life with the testimony of Jesus, to fill my heart with love for my true Savior and to empty my heart of love for my false idols.

Immerse me again and again in the knowledge of the Spirit's power and wisdom in the face of my weakness and ignorance,

So that I will entrust all matters to you, who will work all things for my good and for Christ's glory.

Hear now the petitions that I offer for the sake of my Savior:

(Offer personal petitions here.)

By your Spirit, conform these prayers to your will and by these prayers transform my world according to your will.

I pray in Jesus' name, amen."[12]

---

12 Bryan Chapell, *Praying Backwards: Transform Your Prayer Life by Beginning in Jesus' Name* (Grand Rapids, MI: Baker Books, 2005), 83–84.

Part 3

Presenting
Ourselves to God for
Supernatural Living

*L*IFE ON THE ALTAR brings transformation. Because of our redemption in Christ, believers are in the process of being changed by God's mercies. Our lives need to rise above the status quo of the world's acceptable behavior, because our salvation should impact how we relate with others. We are called to "be imitators of God as beloved children" (Eph. 5:2).

In Part 3, we further focus on Paul's instructions for Life on the Altar. Beginning in Romans 12:9 through the end of the chapter, there are a series of brief, abrupt commands on how we are to live with others, which are nothing short of supernatural living. This section mirrors the themes in the Sermon on the Mount (Matt. 5–7). These directives are impossible to obey without God empowering us. This is the very life that Jesus called us to live. It is the fruit that comes when we present ourselves to God, and it is the most compelling witness we can give.

In Chapter 10, we will focus on living for God's applause in a world with different values. How do we live as "salt and light" in this world (Matt. 5:13–16)? What evidence do we give of a Christ-centered life, and why does it matter? How does God want us to live through the difficult trials we face? These questions lead us to basic, yet profound teachings on what it means to be a Christian.

Chapter 11 takes us through several commands that Paul mentions to guide us when pain and suffering knock upon our door. These unwelcomed intruders can break our spirit if we are not focused on processing affliction with God's power and from His viewpoint. Paul identifies several sources of pain and points us to God's grace and justice as a resting place in the blows of life.

Chapter 12 will give guidance on how to live for Christ when enemies and persecution press in upon us. In contrast to the revenge culture that operates all around us, our calling as followers of Christ is radically different. Apart from a surrendered life to Christ, a life presented to Him, we could never treat our enemies in the way set forth in this chapter.

Chapter 13 will close Part 3 with a look at the challenge of living in a "cancel culture." This is nothing new for the church. For twenty-one centuries, the church has experienced times of severe rejection by the powers that be. While canceled on earth, we are assured we are never canceled by the One who has redeemed us.

Living for God's Approval

"Be imitators of God as beloved children."
Ephesians 5:2

"Let your light shine before others, so that they
may see your good works and give glory to your
Father who is in heaven." Matthew 5:16

IN THE LAST DAYS of his life, Mark Twain wrote in a letter to a friend, "You go to heaven if you want to, I'd rather stay here [in Bermuda]."[1] Obviously, Twain was taken by the beauty of that unique, subtropical island which he visited at least seven times in his life. For him, the biblical promises of heaven were dim by comparison. Twain's words, spoken 150 years ago, represent the mindset of many who would rather have the beauties and riches of this world compared to the promises of Christ found in the gospel. The reality is that a person can't stay in Bermuda or anywhere else on this dying planet, beyond his appointed days.

---

1   Donald Hoffman, *Mark Twain in Paradise: His Voyages to Bermuda* (Columbia, MO: University of Missouri Press, 2006), 1.

The offerings of this age are certainly alluring. It was no small temptation when Satan showed Jesus all the kingdoms of the world and pledged to give them if Christ would bow down and worship him. The temptation was gripping, because the evil one had the ability, in a temporal sense, to make such an offer. It was an appeal for the ultimate power grab, but to this offer Jesus said, "Be gone, Satan! For it is written, 'You shall worship the Lord your God and him only shall you serve'" (Matt. 4:10).

The New Testament affirms that Christ was tempted in every way as we are, yet never buckled to sin's sway (Heb. 4:15). He was completely given to the glory of the Father, and the biblical record testifies that He fulfilled the mission perfectly (John 8:29). Jesus lived an Altar Life before the Father and always did what pleased Him (Matt. 17:5). If we follow Christ, we are called "to walk in the same way in which He walked" (1 John 2:6).

Jesus' teachings in the gospels are nothing short of radical. Jesus requires everything of us. Consider the terms given in Luke 9 for anyone who would want to follow Christ:

> **If anyone would come after me, let him deny himself and take up his cross daily and follow me. For whoever would save his life will lose it, but whoever loses his life for my sake will save it. For what does it profit a man if he gains the whole world and loses or forfeits himself? For whoever is ashamed of me and of my words, of him will the Son of Man be ashamed when he comes in his glory and the glory of the Father and of the holy angels. (Luke 9:23–26)**

Jesus called every would-be follower to deny self, die daily, live obediently to a new master, delight in God's commands, deny the clamor of the world's offerings and live for the glory of another. Each of these commands grates against our fallen nature. This is not a message we would choose to win followers, but then again, we weren't asked!

If we take this passage seriously, we understand why Bermuda looks so good to many. We understand why the rich young ruler walked away from Christ "sorrowful, for he had great possessions" (Mark 10:22). We understand why the crowds, once enthusiastic about Jesus, no longer walked with Him as His message became offensive (John 6:66). We understand the apostle John's tongue twister describing those who defect from following Christ: "They went out from us, but they were not of us; for if they had been of us, they would have continued with us. But they went out, that it might become plain that they all are not of us" (1 John 2:19).

These words sober us before they liberate us. These words devastate us before they deliver us. The pull of the wide and broad road of destruction is great and can only be circumvented by the grace of Jesus. We are tempted to ask, "Who would want to hear this message?" And the answer is at the heart of the gospel: the good news that is proclaimed among the competing ideas of this world is the only way to know God's salvation.

However, for those who have come to know and love the Lord Jesus Christ, we see Him as our only hope in a world that is passing away, present beauty and thrills notwithstanding. We see in the claims of the gospel that Christ is the only One qualified to be our all-sufficient Savior. His substitutionary death is the only sacrifice powerful enough to pay for sin's devastation, and His resurrection proves that He was who He said He was. Consequently, He is worthy of our full allegiance.

A large contingent of humanity is betting that this world is all there is, but that is a bad wager. We know intuitively that there is more to life than what we see. Scripture teaches that God has put eternity in our hearts (Eccl. 3:10). Yet, we fail to live with an eternal perspective. Consequently, the pleasures on earth become the passions of our lives.

We are called to live for another King and to seek His kingdom as the primary drive of our lives in this world. In short, we are called to live a supernatural life by presenting ourselves to God as living sacrifices.

A Life That Pleases God

Some of the blessings that come from Life on the Altar are an inner peace and a confidence. In the daily rhythms of life, as we face decisions and make commitments, we can "prove what the will of God is, that which is good and acceptable and perfect" (Rom.12:2). Believers in Christ have access to this great God who reigns over the universe and is bringing history to completion in Him. Our calling in Jesus is to live for His approval.

Romans 12:9–21 helps set our course to pursue character qualities that please God the Father. We often find in Scripture a list of virtues that we are to seek to attain juxtaposed with behavior that we are to put out of our lives.[2] Paul's list in Romans 12:9–21 is no different as he presents behaviors that should be embraced by every follower of Christ. While these virtues are

2   Eph. 4:25–32; Col. 3:5–10, 12–14; 1 Tim. 3:1–7; 2 Pet. 1:3–10.

common, they are nevertheless supernatural because we cannot live this way in our own strength and power. To present ourselves to God as living sacrifices brings forth an otherworldly witness that flows from us when we build our lives on the gospel.

Being Salt and Light in the Details of Life

The commands and directives found in Romans 12:9–21 remind us of Jesus' signature teaching in the Sermon on the Mount found in Matthew 5–7. There, Jesus set forth how we are to live as citizens of the kingdom of God. Jesus began the sermon with a section called "the Beatitudes" which describe the character and the attitude Christians should emulate. The Beatitudes parallel many of the commands given by Paul in Romans 12 (see Matthew 5:3–12).

Like salt in the ancient world, our witness is to have a preserving effect that reflects the light of Christ which dwells within every believer. We are to shine before others with good works done with virtuous character. We were created to live this way to point others to the Father to whom all glory belongs (Eph. 2:10). Let's consider some examples of virtues that make us the salt and light Jesus admonished His followers to be.

Pursuing Love and Hating Evil

As we mentioned in Chapter 7, our lives are to be marked by sincere love for others, especially brotherly affection for those in the family of God. Paul begins this section by stating, "Let love be genuine. Abhor what is evil; hold fast to what is good. Love one another with brotherly affection. Outdo one another in showing honor" (Rom. 12:9–10). In the Sermon on the Mount, Jesus taught not only that we should love our neighbors, but by His command, we should "love our enemies and pray for those who persecute [us], so that [we] may be sons of [our]Father who is in heaven" (Matt. 5:43–45). Jesus taught and demonstrated this. From the cross He cried, "Father, forgive them, for they know not what they do" (Luke 23:34). This is not how we naturally respond to our enemies, but this is the supernatural living to which we are called.

Fervent in Spirit, Serving the Lord

Next, Paul wrote, "Do not be slothful in zeal, be fervent in spirit, serve the Lord" (Rom. 12:11). The Christian life is not an idle undertaking. A call to zeal in our service means that there is a sense of urgency. Jesus said those "who hunger and thirst for righteousness" are blessed, "for they shall be satisfied" (Matt. 5:6). Our lives are to be marked by zeal for God's agenda—living for what is right according to God and His ways. We are to make the most of every opportunity God gives us to do what He has said is right.

We Are a Hopeful People

Romans 12:12 includes three commands that flow together: "Rejoice in hope, be patient in tribulation, be constant in prayer." They offer direction for living in a dark world fraught with pain and problems. Even though difficulties and sorrows may beset us, we are instructed to rejoice in hope.

In 2009 on *Britain's Got Talent*, Susan Boyle, a 47-year-old woman who was plain by any standards, stood before a crowd of doubters and scoffers. Yet, by the end of her song, she had brought the audience to cheers and tears by the sound of her voice. We love to watch the underdog climb to the top, and Susan Boyle certainly did that with her singing.

Boyle's popularity was also due to the emotional pull of the song she sang, "I Dreamed a Dream" from *Les Miserables*. The song resonates with the human experience, as it speaks of dreams that are dashed and hope that is extinguished. The lyrics are universal and timeless in describing the bitter fallout of sin's curse. This could very well have been Adam and Eve's song, as they were the first to taste of hope torn apart and dreams turned to shame. The unfolding of human history bears witness to this horror and, honestly, every one of us can weigh-in on this reality.

We see it and hear it all around us:
- Like the father who said to his son, "You are nothing but the product of a one-night stand!"
- Where loose ends, irreconcilable relationships, and unending bitterness pass from one generation to the next.
- Where "if only" seems to be the refrain of many living in the backwash of failure, grief, and pain.

Sin is the great life-destroyer, separating us from God and troubling every human relationship; it is behind every broken marriage, every abusive home, every shattered friendship, every evil thought, every evil word, evil deed, every good deed undone, every good word unsaid. We, as a race, are sinners by nature and by choice.

Christians are to rejoice in hope because we know the true Hope Giver. The promises of Christ are sturdy, and His compassion is great. Life on the Altar follows the command in Romans 12:12 to "rejoice in hope." We have been rescued from despair by the hope found in Christ, and we are called as His followers to exude hope, even in the face of persecution and sorrow. Jesus said, "Rejoice and be glad, for your reward is great in heaven" (Matt. 5:12). This is supernatural living and impossible apart from God's power flowing in us and through us as we surrender to Him daily on His altar.

Patient in Tribulation

In addition to being hopeful, we are called to be patient in the pressures of life. The word "tribulation" in Romans 12:12 comes from the Greek word *thlipsis* which means "to crush, press, squeeze," and describes the troubles and trials of life. The apostle James instructed his readers to "count it all joy, my brothers, when you meet trials of various kinds" (Jas. 1:2). When pressed and squeezed, we are called to bear this patiently knowing that God is working on our behalf and conforming us into the image of His Son.

Constant in Prayer

Prayer is the spiritual lifeline for the believer. Jesus said that we should always pray and not lose heart (Luke 18:1). Through adversity, the Lord deepens our lives, as we learn to persevere through difficulties, when we have nowhere to turn but to Him. Our prayer life is a true indicator of our spiritual health. In

Matthew 6:9–13, Jesus gave a model prayer to show us how to relate to the Father. Jesus lived a life of constant prayer, and so should we.

When I was a new believer, I learned that I could pray with my eyes open. With our eyes opened or closed, in the gathering of the church, or in the quiet places of our lives, may we be men and women constant in prayer.

Generosity and Showing Hospitality

In His teaching, Jesus emphasized the importance of generosity and hospitality. His parable of the Good Samaritan captures the true heart of ministry (Luke 10:25–37). Likewise, in the Sermon on the Mount, Jesus called for ministry to the needy to be done in the same manner (Matt. 6:1–4).

Early believers faced harsh circumstances because of their faith. Often, their survival depended upon the generosity and hospitality of fellow believers. However, these are not disciplines confined to the first century. If we look attentively, we will see opportunities to meet pressing needs.

Alexander Strauch in his valuable book, *The Hospitality Commands*, shared this convicting story of a lost opportunity that I fear is all too common among us:

> An elderly single woman, who now attends our church related an experience to me that dramatically illustrates why we need fresh teaching on the subject of Christian hospitality. At one time in her life, she had to travel more than an hour by bus every Sunday to attend a small suburban church. Each week after the Sunday morning service, she would eat alone

in a restaurant and then spend the entire afternoon in a park or library so that she could attend the evening service. She did this for four years. What left her with sour memories of this church was the fact that in four years no one invited her home to eat a Sunday afternoon meal or to rest. It wasn't until she announced she was leaving that an elderly woman in the church invited her home for a meal on her final Sunday.[3]

Strauch followed with this charge: "We need to awaken Christians to their scriptural duty to practice hospitality. We need to show the rich blessings that await all who practice hospitality. We need a fresh vision of hospitality's potential for strengthening our churches and for reaching our neighbors and friends with the gospel."[4]

Paul's list of commands in Romans 12:9–21 also includes suffering (vv. 14–15), humility (v. 16), love for enemies (vv. 19–20), and overcoming evil with good (v. 21). I will pick up these themes in the next few chapters, but I want to mention one other theme prominent in both Romans 12 and the Sermon on the Mount to close out this chapter.

We Are Called to Be Peacemakers

In Matthew 5, Jesus said, "Blessed are the peacemakers, for they shall be called sons of God" (v. 9). In Christ, we have received peace with God through the blood of His cross (Col. 1:20). We

---

3   Alexander Strauch, *The Hospitality Commands* (Littleton, CO: Lewis & Roth Publishers, 1993), 5.

4   Ibid, 7.

have passed from being enemies of God to being received as dear children. Our warfare with Him due to our sin is over, and having received peace from Him, we are to bring peace to others. This peace comes through the gospel and obedience to His Word.

Paul urges believers to bring peace into every relationship. He writes, "Live in harmony with one another ... Repay no one evil for evil but give thought to do what is honorable in the sight of all.... If possible, so far as it depends on you, live peaceably with all" (Rom. 12:16a, 17–18). We are to be emissaries of the Prince of Peace, and as His commissioned ambassadors, we are to give witness that we are God's children.

Furthermore, we should avoid evil retaliation and give our best efforts to live peaceably with others. Again, this is a tall order in a fallen world that is filled with grievances, litigation, divorce, and petty arguments. How do we live above the fray? How do we pray for God's will to be done on earth as it is in heaven? At present, are you at war with someone? How are you processing the conflict?

Pursuing peace is easier said than done. Not only do we have to do battle with our flesh which often screams for retaliation, but we live in a world that tends to walk over the peacemaker types. The key to being a peacemaker is to see this ministry as one that brings the peace of the gospel to troubled relationships. John MacArthur's comments provide important clarity:

> The peace of which Christ speaks in this beatitude, and about which the rest of Scripture speaks, is unlike that which the world knows and strives for. God's peace has nothing to do with politics, armies

and navies, forums of nations, or even councils of churches. It has nothing to do with statesmanship, no matter how great, or with arbitration, compromise, negotiated truces, or treaties. God's peace, the peace of which the Bible speaks, never evades issues; it knows nothing of peace at any price. It does not gloss or hide, rationalize or excuse. It confronts problems and seeks to solve them, and after the problems are solved it builds a bridge between those who were separated by the problems. It often brings its own struggle, pain, hardship, and anguish, because such are often the price of healing. It is not a peace that will be brought by kings, presidents, prime ministers, diplomats, or international humanitarians. It is the inner personal peace that only He can give to the soul of man and that only His children can exemplify.[5]

This is supernatural living as God's peace flows from our once war-torn hearts into a world still at war with Him. May this chapter be an encouragement to look at the truths in Romans 12 to quiet your heart and rest in God's guidance.

Suing Saints

Viewing billboards during highway travel can be an informative cultural indicator. You don't have to travel far to see the glut of attorney advertisements along the interstates. If I were a visitor from another culture, billboards and television commercials

---

5   John F. MacArthur, *Matthew 1–7* in *The MacArthur New Testament Commentary* (Winona Lake, IN: BMH Books, 1985), 210.

would indicate that having an aggressive attorney is one of the most important resources that I could have.

We live in a lawsuit-crazed culture where advertisements for attorney services appeal to your right to file a suit against another. The appeals are incredible and at times shameless: "Have you got your check yet?" "I love my lawyer!" "After you have been injured, there's only one place to turn…." "I will fight for you!"

An attorney is often the first person someone calls after any scrape or conflict. Without question, there are times and circumstances when an attorney is needed. For the Christian, however, there are many things to consider before seeking legal counsel, especially when it pertains to another believer.

In 1 Corinthians 6, the apostle Paul addressed another problem in the Corinthian congregation. These believers were in the practice of launching lawsuits against each other. They were taking their personal grievances against one another and airing them out in the city's courts.

Paul was not attacking the courts (Rom. 13:1–7). His concern was with believers who use the court system as a platform for their grievances against one another. This was and is a devastating practice because the witness of Christ is taken into the mud. Instead, through the Scriptures, God has made a better way for His people to handle their conflicts with each other.

When Grievances Come Among Believers

In Corinth, the culture had soaked into the fabric of the church in two crippling ways. The church's witness was plagued by sexual immorality (1 Cor. 5) and by forbidden lawsuits (1 Cor. 6:1–8).

Paul argues that because of their destiny in Christ, namely, to rule and reign with Him, couldn't they find someone in the church to help mediate their disputes? The question begs for an affirmative answer—yes!

From our destiny in Christ, Paul moves to a practical consideration in dealing with all temporal matters by asking the question, "Is it really worth it?" If believers' lives are to reflect God's grace and glory, shouldn't we be willing to take a loss rather than insist on our rights by filing a lawsuit against another believer?

I realize there are a thousand contingencies that come to mind, and many should be considered, but the driving conviction as it relates to our response to another believer should be to honor Christ and love the brethren. Many decisions in the Christian life are beyond simple answers and require a prayerful reflection on deeper questions:

- How would Christ be most glorified in this decision before me?
- What's Jesus calling me to do?
- What's at stake if I press forward?
- Would it be best to take a loss? To be defrauded, and trust instead in God's record keeping? Does this issue demand that I take a stand for righteousness' sake?

Since followers of Christ are called to live otherworldly, counter-culturally, and kingdom-mindedly, then seeking reconciliation would be a refreshing response in the present climate. The testimony of Christ should be uppermost in our minds. We should look to the One who is an amazing demonstration of grace and became poor so that by His poverty, we might become rich (2 Cor. 8:9).

Well Done, Good and Faithful Servant!

Living for God's approval is not a quest to earn salvation as if we are earning merit badges in a scouting program. We can only be forgiven by His grace through Jesus Christ. Life on the Altar means presenting ourselves to God to live in a way that pleases Him. We are living for His applause.

Jesus alludes to that truth in the Parable of the Talents. In this parable, Jesus described the scene of a master returning after a journey to settle with his servants whom he had entrusted with funds. Two of the servants had invested their talents and, consequently, increased the investment. The master said to each of them, "Well done, good and faithful servant" (Matt. 25:21, 23). Jesus' point in the parable was to challenge every believer to invest wisely in the life that God has given us and live in such a way as to hear at the end of it all, "Well done, well done indeed!"

In Cairo, Egypt, there is a graveyard for American missionaries. One of those sun-scorched tombstones reads, "William Borden, 1887–1913." Randy Alcorn, who visited that cemetery, describes Borden as one who lived on the altar for God's approval. Alcorn writes,

> Borden, a Yale graduate and heir to great wealth, rejected a life of ease in order to bring the gospel to Muslims. Refusing even to buy himself a car, Borden gave away hundreds of thousands of dollars to missions. After only four months of zealous ministry in Egypt, he contracted spinal meningitis

and died at age twenty-five. On the grave marker are some notes describing his love and sacrifices for the kingdom of God and for Muslim people ending with this inscription: "Apart from faith in Christ, there is no explanation for such a life."[6]

Disagreements and grievances inside and outside of the church will come. But living Life on the Altar empowers us to live as Christ lived and for the commendation of our heavenly Father—which is the ultimate reward.

Altar Moments

1. Do you struggle with the idea that you can live a life that pleases God? How could a regular review of Romans 12:1–21 provide light on how to live for God's approval?

2. Did you see the connection and similarities between the Sermon on the Mount (Matt. 5–7) and Romans 12:9–21? How does this give clarity and focus for living the Christian life?

3. We are called as Christians to live in harmony with one another. Why is that so difficult? What counsel do you receive about contributing to the peace and harmony in: your marriage? your family? your church? your community? your workplace?

---

6   Randy Alcorn, *The Treasure Principle* (Colorado Springs, CO: Multnomah Books 2001), 34–35.

Prayer:

Dear Lord,

I receive Your Word as authoritative in my life, and I have found in Romans 12 that You have much to say about how I treat others. Keep me from separating my treatment of others from my relationship with You, as if they were competing interests. Help me to love what You love. Help me to be a peacemaker that stands upon truth, walks in humility, and promotes the peace of Christ in every relationship of my life. May I never forget that You delight when Your people dwell in love and unity (Psa. 133:1), and it was Your prayer that we would be one as You and the Father are one (John 17:11).

In the Name of the Prince of Peace, Amen.

Chapter 11

When Pain Knocks upon My Door

"Weep with those who weep." Romans 12:15

"Jesus wept." John 11:35

ONE OF THE STRONGEST apologetics to commend the reality of the Christian faith is that we have a Savior who wept at the grave of a dear friend. John 11 takes us to Bethany, a sleepy village two miles removed from Jerusalem. Jesus visited Bethany regularly to spend time with His friends Mary, Martha, and Lazarus. In John 11 their home was not a peaceful setting. It was the scene of deep concern because Lazarus was deathly sick. In desperation, Mary and Martha sent for Jesus saying, "Lord, he whom you love is ill" (v. 3). Confident that He would come, they called Jesus, but He didn't come. He delayed two days. In verse 5, we learn that the delay was not from neglect for "Jesus loved Martha and her sister and Lazarus." So why did Jesus not rush immediately to Bethany?

Two reasons emerge. The first, according to v. 4, was "for the glory of God, so that the Son of God may be glorified through it." A second reason was for the disciples to believe that Jesus was the Son of God, the One who would give them eternal life (v. 15).

Far from being a God who is incapable of handling the blows of life, even death itself, we find an interesting contrast. The reference to Jesus weeping at the tomb of Lazarus is also the setting for one of Jesus' "I Am" statements.[1] In this case, Jesus claimed to be Lord over life and death. He said to Martha, "I am the resurrection and the life. Whoever believes in me, though he die, yet shall he live, and everyone who lives and believes in me shall never die. Do you believe this?" (John 11:25–26).

Is that not an incredible statement? Who speaks in those terms? Who would dare make a statement like that unless they were making a claim to be God? When Jesus finally arrived in Bethany, Lazarus had died, and he had been in the tomb for four days. When Christ comes into the village, it brings a reaction from Martha and Mary both saying to Him in different conversations, "Lord, if you had been here, my brother would not have died" (John 11:21, 32). Do you think they had been discussing why Jesus delayed?

Who can blame them?

---

1   John recorded seven "I AM" statements which gave witness that Jesus was God and Messiah: "I am the bread of life" (John 6:35); "I am the light of the world" (8:12); "I am the door of the sheep" (10:7, 9); "I am the good shepherd" (10:11, 14); "I am the resurrection and the life" (11:25); "I am the way, and the truth, and the life" (14:6); "I am the true vine" (15:1).

"If only Jesus had been here," sounds a lot like, "Why did God let this happen?" We all struggle with questions and fault-finding when life hurts:

- If only I hadn't moved here.
- If only I hadn't married him.
- If only I had listened to her.
- If only I hadn't gone to that college.
- If only I hadn't gone on that date or taken that job.

Such questions have no resolve.

One man shared with me the events surrounding his teen-aged daughter's death. She went to run an errand one night, an errand that turned out to be unnecessary, and she was killed when a semi-truck hit her car head on. An answer to why things go wrong may never be resolved in this life, but that does not mean that we can't find rest from the questions that plague us.

Martha needed to know that Jesus was in control, and Mary needed to know that Jesus was not indifferent to their need. We share those same needs when pain comes knocking upon our door. Tears flowed in Bethany on that day. John records the raw grief, saying, "When Jesus saw her weeping, and the Jews who had come with her also weeping, he was deeply moved in his spirit and greatly troubled. And he said, 'Where have you laid him?' They said to him, 'Lord, come and see.' Jesus wept" (John 11:33–35).

Why did Jesus weep? Was it because He would never enjoy fellowship with Lazarus again? No, because Jesus would soon call him from the grave, and Lazarus would live until his death. Was it because Jesus had met His match with the finality of death? No, because of His promise to Martha that He was the resurrection and the life and that one could have life beyond the grave through faith in Him (v. 25). I believe Jesus wept because He saw the devastating effects of sin upon human beings, and especially upon His close friends. Since the Fall (Gen. 3), sin has brought death, pain, and tears. The hope of the gospel brings us to a Savior who is in control and who cares deeply as we walk through the valley of suffering (Psa. 23:4). The tears of this world are not the final word, for God has promised a day when every tear will be wiped away and death will be no more (Rev. 21:4).

Roused by God's Megaphone

In his book *The Problem of Pain*, C. S. Lewis wrote, "God whispers to us in our pleasures, speaks in our conscience, but shouts in our pains: it is His megaphone to rouse a deaf world."[2] Pain gets our attention like an alarm that awakens us to difficult realities of life—the death of a loved one, the betrayal of a friend, the shattering of marriage vows, the collapse of a nation, the trauma of violent crime, the devastation of natural disasters, and thousands of other heartbreaks that fill this groaning planet. We don't have to look far to find suffering, and we can be sure that one day pain will come knocking at our door.

Gratefully, the hope found in God's Word has not left us in the lurch regarding the suffering of this life. We find in Scripture that suffering is promised, and we also find precious assurances that God is with us through it all. The psalmist declared with

---

2   C. S. Lewis, *The Problem of Pain* (New York: HarperOne, 2009), 59, Kindle edition.

confidence, "The Lord is near to the brokenhearted and saves the crushed in spirit. Many are the afflictions of the righteous, but the Lord delivers him out of them all" (Psa. 34:18–19).

The whole prospect of following Jesus Christ is a call to die to self. Life on the Altar is a picture of dying to self for the sake of God's kingdom. In yet another paradox, our dying to self, our presenting ourselves to God as living sacrifices, becomes the pathway by which we truly live as God intended. This life in Christ brings not only promised joy and peace but continues forever and ever. This eternal perspective becomes the ballast that keeps us steadied in times of pain.

Paul describes the believer's hope when pain comes: "For I consider that the sufferings of this present time are not worth comparing with the glory that is to be revealed to us" (Rom. 8:18). When pain comes knocking at our door, our union with Christ offers hope when all seems pointless. Through every trial, we are being conformed into the image of Jesus Christ (Rom. 8:29). Charles Swindoll writes of the sanctifying work of pain in the believer's life:

> Pain humbles the proud. It softens the stubborn. It melts the hard. Silently and relentlessly, it wins battles deep within the lonely soul … Pain operates alone; it needs no assistance. It communicates its own message whether to statesman or servant, preacher or prodigal, mother or child. By staying, it refuses to be ignored. By hurting, it reduces its victim to profound depths of anguish. And it is at that anguishing point that the sufferer either submits and learns, developing maturity and character; or

resists and becomes embittered, swamped by self-pity; smothered by self-will … I have tried and I cannot find, either in Scripture or history; a strong-willed individual whom God used greatly until He allowed him to be hurt deeply.[3]

As we have been following the apostle Paul's application of the gospel in the life of the believer, Life on the Altar involves living with pain and suffering. Not only does this include our own personal encounters with sorrows, but it also involves bearing one another's burdens. Patiently enduring trials and compassionately caring for others is a witness in this world. Paul mentions in Romans 12:15 that we should "weep with those who weep."

We are talking in this section of the book about supernatural living. We mistakenly envision such living as being heroic like a character in the Marvel Universe. However, this is not the picture given at all. God's power is on display through what the world would dismiss as weak and foolish. When God's people show care and compassion as an expression of God's love *that* is supernatural living.

Weep with Those Who Weep

In the life of any church there are great joys and heartbreaks. Spending nearly three decades with one congregation brings the full spectrum of life experiences. We have celebrated God's goodness on so many fronts, rejoicing with those who rejoice in the birth of babies, the celebration of weddings, the recognition

---

3   Charles R. Swindoll, *Come Before Winter … and Share My Hope* (Portland: Multnomah Press, 1985), 151–52.

of anniversaries, along with spiritual growth seen in baptisms and changed lives through the gospel.

Heartaches have been a reality as well, and we have had many occasions to weep with those who weep. In March of 1999, pain knocked upon our door through the tragic death of Mildred Vessel. Mildred had served as a long-time nursery worker at FBCG, and an entire generation of children, including my oldest three children, were introduced to church life in the loving arms of that dear woman. Mildred's daughter, Karla Miller, also served alongside her.

On Wednesday, March 10, 1999, after our evening ministries, Mildred and Karla left FBCG and were gunned down. Mildred was shot and killed in front of her home. Karla and her son were shot along with others at their church. The shooter was Karla's estranged husband who approached the pew where his two-year-old son sat. The little boy said, "Daddy!" These would be his last words as his father looked at him and shot him along with his mother in a once peaceful sanctuary.

In the aftermath, FBCG was able to host the funeral, which provided an important connection in our town as we wept with those who wept. Through the years, I still have conversations about that funeral with people in our community. We experienced an outpouring of God's grace, as we grieved the manifest evil that brought about these murders. Our comfort was found in the promises of Christ. We were reminded that He is still in control, that He cares, and that the final word awaits to be given when He returns.

A Lady Named "Katrina"

On Sunday, August 28th, 2005, we gathered as a church for worship with a foreboding outlook on the next 24 hours. The radar revealed a monster roaring through the Gulf of Mexico, and we were right in the projected path of a catastrophic hurricane. As we closed the worship service, I addressed the congregation by stating the obvious, namely that the radar and forecast were troubling, and that we should make final decisions regarding the storm. After my closing comments, we prayed for God's protection and provision. I shared with our church that Hurricane Katrina promised to be a future pseudonym for disaster, and I was confident that it would change South Louisiana in a very profound way. I challenged our people that with such destruction coming, we could count on unprecedented opportunities for ministry.

The next day Hurricane Katrina battered the Gulf Coast. When all was said and done, there were 1,833 deaths and $108 billion in damage. In his comprehensive and impressive chronicle on the catastrophe of Hurricane Katrina, Douglas Brinkley wrote, "The storm-surge flooding, which submerged a half million homes, creating the largest domestic refugee crisis since the Civil War. Eighty percent of New Orleans was under water, as debris and sewage coursed through the streets, and whole towns in southeastern Louisiana ceased to exist."[4]

Gonzales, being some 60 miles west of New Orleans along the route of Interstate 10, would escape the higher winds and

---

4   Douglas Brinkley, *The Great Deluge: Hurricane Katrina, New Orleans, and the Mississippi Gulf Coast* (New York: William Morrow Publishers, 2006), Cover.

the flooding of our friends in New Orleans. However, as one of the first major exits out of New Orleans, we became a city of refuge for many fleeing Katrina. The week following the hurricane seemed apocalyptic. Our community swelled to twice its population, and the infrastructure was unable to accommodate the surge of people. I remember going into Walmart the week after the storm and seeing the shelves virtually empty. The line to check out, if you could find any supplies, extended to the back of the store with an estimated 45-minute wait.

Our church had tremendous opportunities to minister to hundreds of people. The storm brought a remarkable connection as local government, volunteer organizations, and churches banded together to meet pressing needs. It was overwhelming to receive support from around the United States. I will always be grateful for ministry partners who sent significant financial gifts and entrusted us to invest these resources on the front lines of human suffering. Those who came to our church for assistance heard the good news of Jesus Christ. We offered to pray with each one, and without exception, it was received gladly.

FBCG became a clearinghouse to put resources and hope into the lives of many. The stories of those brought to us from New Orleans, and the surrounding area, will always be etched in my mind. I remember the man from St. Bernard parish who said to me in tears that his wife had insisted that he put an axe in his attic prior to the storm. His only way of escape was to chop through their roof, and from their roof they were rescued by boat. He told me with great emotion that he was so glad he listened to her, or they would have drowned in their home.

Those days and weeks after the storm were a season of sorrow and loss but also of redemption and new beginnings. It seems like God is always bringing us through these great realities of life. We live in a fractured world where pain abounds. It has been said that if tears were indelible ink, we would all be stained forever. With grief and sorrows found in every home and highway, every school and subdivision, every neighborhood and nation, what comfort can we find?

Recovering Lament

Mark Vroegop in his book, *Dark Clouds, Deep Mercy,* writes,

> Lament is how we bring our sorrow to God. Without lament we won't know how to process pain. Silence, bitterness, and even anger can dominate our spiritual lives instead. Without lament we won't know how to help people walking through sorrow. Instead, we'll offer trite solutions, unhelpful comments, or impatient responses.... Lament is how Christians grieve. It is how to help hurting people. Lament is how we learn important truths about God and our world. My personal and pastoral experience has convinced me that biblical lament is not only a gift but also a neglected dimension of the Christian life for many twenty-first-century Christians.[5]

Vroegop concludes, "Christianity is unbalanced and limited in the hope we offer if we neglect this minor-key song. We

---

5 Mark Vroegop, *Dark Clouds, Deep Mercy: Discovering the Grace of Lament* (Wheaton, Crossway, 2019), 21.

need to recover the ancient practice of lament and the grace that comes through it. Christianity suffers when lament is missing."[6]

Weeping alongside and comforting those who mourn does not come easily for many of us. Lament makes us uncomfortable. Mourning is often viewed as weakness that shouldn't be expressed in polite company. Corporate worship is never considered in a minor-key, because it is too much of a downer and will chase away the visitors. "Let's keep it positive and chipper" is the prevailing philosophy of ministry. However, this approach to life and ministry defies reality. Life is not lived exclusively in the heights. We all must walk through valleys that are dark. In these valleys, one of the strongest assurances of God's presence is the support we receive from others who weep with us.

Ministry to hurting people is not complicated. If we will embrace the simple command to "weep with those who weep," our presence and our care will mirror a heart of compassion. You don't need a counseling degree to minister to hurting people, just a heart to help bear their sorrows.

He Is with Us Always

Martha Snell Nicholson in her poem "Guests" holds out the promise of God's presence in times of pain:

> Pain knocked upon my door and said
> That she had come to stay,
> And though I would not welcome her
> But bade her go away,
> She entered in.
> Like my own shade

---

6   Ibid.

She followed after me,
And from her stabbing, stinging sword
No moment was I free.
And then one day another knocked
Most gently at my door.
I cried, "No, Pain is living here,
There is not room for more."
And then I heard His tender voice,
"'Tis I, be not afraid."
And from the day He entered in,
The difference it made![7]

Yes, that is true! Christ makes all the difference, and He will in no way cast out all who come to Him (John 6:37). He heals the brokenhearted and binds up their wounds (Psa. 147:3). He is the One to whom we must go in times of pain, for He has what we need most, the words of eternal life (John 6:66).

Scripture holds up Christ, who endured the cross and rose triumphantly from the grave, as the One who pledges to be with us until we are in His very presence. Jude conveys the power of Christ in a believer's life in what has become my favorite benediction in the Bible: "Now to him who is able to keep you from stumbling and to present you blameless before the presence of his glory with great joy, to the only God, our Savior, through Jesus Christ our Lord, be glory, majesty, dominion, and authority, before all time and now and forever. Amen" (Jude 24–25). Dear believer in Jesus, rest in His strong grip upon your life. He will hold you fast no matter what comes.

---

7   Martha Snell Nicholson, "Guests," quoted in Swindoll, *Come Before Winter*, 152.

Altar Moments

1. Do you agree with the opening sentence of this chapter that one of the strongest defenses of Christianity is that we have a Savior who wept in the face of human suffering? Read Isaiah 53. What does this passage reveal about the suffering of Christ in His role as our sin-bearer?

2. Are you dealing with an "if only" situation in your life? Read John 11:1–44. What comfort can be found in Christ from these verses? How do vv. 25 and 26 offer hope beyond our present grief?

3. What are some practical ways you can support those who are hurting?

Prayer:

Dear Lord, we pray with the psalmist:

"I am continually with you; you hold my right hand. You guide me with your counsel, and afterward you will receive me to glory. Whom have I in heaven but you? And there is nothing on earth that I desire besides you. My flesh and my heart may fail, but God is the strength of my heart and my portion forever. For behold, those who are far from you shall perish; you put an end to everyone who is unfaithful to you. But for me it is good to be near God; I have made the LORD GOD my refuge, that I may tell of all your works" (Psa. 73:23–28). Amen.

Chapter 12

Got an Enemy?

"Bless those who persecute you; bless and do not
curse them." Romans 12:14

"If your enemy is hungry, feed him; if he is thirsty,
give him something to drink; for by so doing you
will heap burning coals on his head."
Romans 12:20

THROUGHOUT ROMANS 12, THE apostle Paul provides
one demonstration after another of how the gospel is to be
worked out in the believer's life. In Part 3, we are discovering
how Altar Life bears witness to the supernatural work of God in
the believer's life. Chapter 11 looked at the pain that comes with
grief and loss. In the next two chapters, we will look at how suffering comes from the blows of enemies.

Got an Enemy?

Do you have an enemy? One who has expressed great hatred
toward you? One who intends to bring injury to you? Like Paul,
do you have an Alexander the coppersmith in your life (2 Tim.

4:14)? If you do, maybe you are struggling with what obedience to Christ looks like in the face of such an adversary.

Charles Spurgeon once gave the following counsel to young pastors, "Get a friend to tell you your faults, or better still, welcome an enemy who will watch you keenly and sting you savagely. What a blessing such an irritating critic will be to a wise man, what an intolerable nuisance to a fool!"[1] At first glance this doesn't sit well. This counsel is ironic because enemies are typically those we want removed from our lives. We want them silenced, not emboldened. They disturb our sleep. They disrupt the equilibrium of our days. Surely, because of the pain they bring, God does not want us to have them, right?

We mistakenly think that enemies are solely the work of the devil, yet they come from God's gracious hand to show us our sin and teach us humility. God uses enemies in a Romans 8:28 fashion for the purpose of conforming us into the image of Christ.

Paul's account of the thorn in the flesh in 2 Corinthians 12 is a good example of God's work through our enemies. This thorn was not a small barb found on a rose bush. Paul uses the word *skólops* which describes something pointed, sharp, like a wooden stake.[2] The term captures the pain that comes from being impaled by a sharp instrument. He describes this stake as "a messenger of Satan" (2 Cor. 12:7).

While much speculation has been given on the nature of Paul's thorn, the most compelling explanation is that it was a

---

1 Charles H. Spurgeon, *Lectures to My Students, Lecture 1–13* (Copyright by Benno Zuiddam, 2013), location 3335, Kindle edition.
2 J. H. Thayer, *A Greek-English Lexicon of the New Testament* (New York: Harper & Brothers, 1889), 579, Logos Bible Software.

person, or persons, with a demonic influence upon the Corinthian church to undermine and destroy Paul's ministry. Paul identifies adversaries who had been operating in the Corinthian church. These enemies had disparaged Paul, saying that he was ugly and that he couldn't preach (2 Cor. 10:10)! I don't care how spiritual you are; comments like that take a toll, especially when you are giving your best to advance the gospel.

Three times Paul asked God for relief from this "thorn," and the request was answered each time with a "No." The comfort given to Paul was that God's grace was sufficient for this agonizing pain. God intended to manifest His strength through Paul's weaknesses (2 Cor. 12:9). This was no small trial for Paul. While the thorn was insufferable, Paul was not without hope, because the Lord strengthened him.

One example of this strengthening grace is found in Acts 18. Paul had begun his work in Corinth and was dealing with fear. One evening, the living, resurrected, and enthroned Christ came to Paul in a vision and said to him, "Do not be afraid, but go on speaking and do not be silent, for I am with you, and no one will attack you to harm you, for I have many in this city who are my people" (Acts 18:9–10). With that word, Paul "stayed a year and six months, teaching the Word of God among them" (v. 11). This demonstrates what it meant when the Lord said that His grace was sufficient for Paul's thorn.

When Paul wrote in Romans 12 that we are to bless those who persecute us and to do good to our enemies, he was writing as one who had many enemies. Yet, he saw the advance of the gospel despite those painful experiences (1 Cor. 16:9). Could our most powerful witness for Christ be through our response to our enemies?

Loving and Praying for Our Enemies

Loving and praying for our enemies is quite an undertaking when their words and actions come like a wrecking ball into our lives. It is hard to love when you know the goal of an adversary is to harm you and your family, or worse. But that is precisely the call for the Christ-follower (Matt. 5:44). This does not mean we are consigned to pacifism. Loving and praying for an enemy includes, if given the opportunity, rebuke, calling them to account through law enforcement for reckless and unlawful conduct, giving self-defense, or seeking legal action.

Even within the body of Christ, application of redemptive church discipline is a loving response to sinful conduct and defection. Paul wrote to Titus, "As for a person who stirs up division, after warning him once and then twice, have nothing more to do with him" (Tit. 3:10). Paul is advocating for the removal of such a brother or sister if they do not repent from their destructive behavior. Loving our enemy may involve distancing ourselves when a healthy relationship is not possible because of their refusal to reconcile (Prov. 14:7; 22:24).

At the heart of Paul's teaching is a call to guard our hearts and minds from the noxious weeds of bitterness, so that if our enemy is hungry or thirsty, we are ready to minister to him or her (Rom. 12:19–21). This is supernatural living, because having an enemy can very easily lead to sinful anger. We need this biblical reinforcement and the power of the Holy Spirit to see clearly through the pain inflicted by our enemies.

Learning and Receiving from Our Enemies

A study of King David's life is amazing on several fronts. From the obscurity of a shepherd boy to national prominence through his slaying of Goliath, his life was far from dull. He was a man of great skill, courage, and warfare. In contrast to his skill on the battlefield, David was also known as the sweet poet and singer of Israel (2 Sam. 23:1).

David's ascension to the throne of Israel made him a magnet for enemies. Many of the psalms express the piercing pain inflicted by his foes and a plea for God's deliverance. The Lord was David's refuge and the One who prepared a table before him in the presence of his enemies (Psa. 23:5).

In 2 Samuel 16, King David could have ended the life of a man named Shimei who cursed the king severely. Shimei said to David, "Get out, get out, you man of bloodshed, and worthless fellow!" (v. 7). This cursing came at the lowest point in David's life, as he and his loyal followers fled Jerusalem because of the betrayal of his son, Absalom. Hearing Shimei's disrespectful rant, Abishai said to David, "Why should this dead dog curse my lord the king? Let me go over and take off his head" (v. 9). Yet, David's response is remarkable, "If the Lord has told him, 'Curse David, then who shall say, "Why have you done so?" … Let him alone and let him curse, for the Lord has told him. Perhaps the Lord will look on my affliction and return good to me instead of his cursing this day'" (vv. 10–12 NASB).

David accepted that his adversary was from the Lord and found comfort in trusting God. We know that David later gave instruction to Solomon regarding Shimei (1 Kgs. 2:8–9), but on this day, David received the verbal blows of his enemy as from the Lord and for his good.

We must remember that we wrestle not against flesh and blood (Eph. 6:12). We daily struggle with the triumvirate of this world's system, the devil, and our personal sin. Our fellow man is not our ultimate enemy. The call of God upon our lives is to live counter-culturally, which includes loving our enemies and doing good to them.

Blessing and Ministering to Our Enemies

Paul's language in Romans 12 is succinct, "Bless those who persecute you; bless and do not curse them" (v. 14). His application of this is explained in verse 20 where Paul says, "If your enemy is hungry, feed him; if he is thirsty, give him something to drink; for by so doing you will heap burning coals on his head."

The first application is seen in the word "bless." To bless our enemies is to be committed to their spiritual good. This must flow from a heart that has been transformed by the gospel. The book of Proverbs gives wisdom pertaining to our attitude toward enemies: "Do not rejoice when your enemy falls, and do not let your heart be glad when he stumbles; or the Lord will see it and be displeased and turn His anger away from him" (Prov. 24:17). This is what it means to bless our enemy.

Consider Paul's treatment of the Philippian jailer in Acts 16 as a compelling example of loving one's enemies. Paul and Silas were in the Philippian jail for proclaiming the gospel. They were incarcerated for doing good and were falsely accused. They were beaten with rods by the city officials and placed in stocks in the inner prison. Yet, notice what Luke tells us happened next:

> **About midnight Paul and Silas were praying and singing hymns to God, and the prisoners were listening to them, and suddenly there was a great earthquake, so that the foundations of the prison were shaken. And immediately all the doors were opened, and everyone's bonds were unfastened. When the jailer woke and saw that the prison doors were open, he drew his sword and was about to kill himself, supposing that the prisoners had escaped. But Paul cried with a loud voice, "Do not harm yourself, for we are all here." (Acts 16:25–28)**

When the doors of the prison were opened by the earthquake, the jailer drew his sword and was preparing to take his life. This was his response because he would have been sentenced to death if any of the prisoners had escaped. He was saving Rome the trouble. It is not hard to imagine that some would have encouraged him to fall on his sword, but not Paul. The reason for Paul's response was so that he could share the gospel with his enemy so that he would not die but truly live in Christ.

If you were treated the way Paul and Silas were treated, would you have responded as Paul did? Paul's ministry to this jailer prevented his suicide and gave Paul the opportunity to share the gospel with him and his family. When the jailer asked Paul and Silas, "Sirs, what must I do to be saved" (Acts 16:30), I imagine that Paul and Silas looked at one another, smiled, and said with no hesitation, "Believe in the Lord Jesus, and you will be saved" (Acts 16:31). Salvation came to that jailor and his family through the love of Paul and Silas. These faithful servants lived their lives surrendered to God on the altar.

However, opportunities to do good to our enemies sometimes break down because it is no longer possible to have civil conversations with them. Some things are so messy that we must conclude that the conflict, as much as we would like it to be resolved, will have to be worked out at the judgment seat. Even so, as much as it depends upon us, we must pursue peace, truth, and love with our enemies (Rom. 12:18).

Second, we can love our enemies by meeting their physical needs. If they are hungry, we are to feed them; if they are thirsty, we are to give them a drink (Rom. 12:20). This kind of response flies in the face of the revenge mindset of our human nature. Vengeance is the attitude du jour, but what may seem right and natural, nevertheless leaves a bitter wake and a blemished testimony for the believer. How we respond to our enemies is really about who we want to please.

Paul stated that by doing good to an enemy we will "heap burning coals on his head" (Rom. 12:20). Meeting an enemy's physical needs may bring shame and regret upon him for his mistreatment, and thus, be a sincere way to his heart, possibly leading to his or her salvation. Believers who live in this way provide an example of the way God has treated us. We were at enmity with Him because of our sin, yet God has given grace to those who don't deserve it (Rom. 5:10).

Earlier, we discussed the paradoxes found in Scripture: doctrines or themes that seem to be in contradiction but are nevertheless true. An important consideration in trying to interpret and apply the Scripture to our lives is to study the different perspectives given throughout the counsel of God's Word. For that reason, I want to say a word about the way the psalmists struggled with their enemies.

Those Imprecatory Psalms

Imprecatory psalms are expressions of deep anguish and anger over the acts of an enemy. King David acknowledged such anger toward his enemies when he wrote, "I hate them with complete hatred; I count them my enemies" (Psa. 139:22).[3] There is no toning down the passion of the imprecatory psalms. Their statements are some of the most troubling in Scripture and seem to be in direct contradiction to the teachings of Jesus and Paul. C. S. Lewis wrote that these psalms strike "us in the face ... like the heat from a furnace mouth."[4]

Can you imagine hearing in the pastoral prayer this Sunday, "Lord, we hate them with a perfect hatred, and we count them our enemies?" We know we are on dangerous ground when we harbor such anger, because our anger never accomplishes the righteousness of God (Jas. 1:20).

However, we are not left to put our hands in the air when we read these psalms. First, these psalms seem to be the response to an offense against God's anointed, the King of Israel. We see

---

3   Imprecatory psalms are prayers that call down curses on one's enemies. Psalms 58, 59, 69, 109, 139.

4   C. S. Lewis, *Reflections on the Psalms* (New York: Inspiration Press, 1987), 142.

this in one of these psalms as the psalmist concludes his imprecation. He does so for the purpose of God's glory and reign, "That they may know that God rules over Jacob to the ends of the earth. Selah" (Psa. 59:12–13).

Second, the psalmist leaves justice in the hands of God. Based upon the injustice, the psalmist calls out for God to act. In Psalm 58 David said, "O God, break the teeth in their mouths; tear out the fangs of the young lions, O LORD (Psa. 58:6)!" David is calling for God to do right considering his enemy's injustices. Likewise, we should desire punishment for evil but trust God with that punishment, remembering that "vengeance is [God's]. He will repay" (Rom. 12:19).

Far from taking matters into his own hands, David pleads with God to act. Conversely, we live in a culture that sees vengeance and retaliation as an expression of good. I have heard people justify their revenge and retaliation by saying, "After all, the Bible says, 'an eye for an eye, and a tooth for a tooth'" (Exod. 21:24). What is left out of their interpretation is that God gave this principle to the nation of Israel, not to individuals. He gave the "eye for an eye" principle to govern Israel's jurisprudence and to establish just and equitable laws. This is not permission to take personal vengeance. We all know why, don't we? Left to ourselves, we would take a head for an eye and a heart for a tooth.

I believe a third consideration with interpreting imprecatory statements is found in Jesus' use of them. In Matthew 11, Jesus speaks "woe" to Chorazin, Bethsaida, and Capernaum. He speaks of judgment to come upon these cities for their wholesale rejection of Christ in their midst. He rebukes them for how they squandered access to God's redemption through their manifest unbelief.

Encouragement for Trials Ahead

Psalm 109 is one of the most emotionally charged of all the imprecatory psalms. After expressing his grievances and curses, the psalmist prays for God's help and deliverance. The psalmist concludes with this word of comfort for those who suffer pain at the hands of enemies, "For he stands at the right hand of the needy one, to save him from those who condemn his soul to death" (Psa. 109:31). In reading that verse, I am drawn to the account of Stephen's stoning in Acts 7.

Stephen was a righteous man who preached to the Sanhedrin about Israel's unbelief. He provided a masterful rebuke of the religious establishment for rejecting Jesus, and his message was met with great hostility. Thus, Stephen's end was inevitable. Read slowly the final moments of his life:

> Now when they heard these things they were enraged, and they ground their teeth at him. But he, full of the Holy Spirit, gazed into heaven and saw the glory of God, and Jesus standing at the right hand of God. And he said, "Behold, I see the heavens opened, and the Son of Man standing at the right hand of God." But they cried out with a loud voice and stopped their ears and rushed together at him. Then they cast him out of the city and stoned him. And the witnesses laid down their garments at the feet of a young man named Saul. And as they were stoning Stephen, he

**called out, "Lord Jesus, receive my spirit." And falling
to his knees he cried out with a loud voice, "Lord, do
not hold this sin against them." And when he had said
this, he fell asleep. (Acts 7:54–60)**

What was true for Stephen, is also true for us, and for all who would live godly in Christ Jesus. Persecution is an unpopular promise but suffering for Christ is at the heart of biblical Christianity. We hear, "God has a wonderful plan for your life," represented as a gospel promise. In one sense that is true; Jesus came that we might have life and have it more abundantly (John 10:10). He came that we might live eternally in Him. What if you are Stephen? Stephen doesn't fit into the typical Western church paradigm of blessing. Stephen didn't see his life as being his own. He was given the task of speaking for Jesus which led to his death, but he was not alone. While he breathed his last in this world, his life was not over.

Imprecatory psalms provide an important balance, as we seek to love our enemies. We read the account of those who have gone before us and are inspired by their struggle to obey God's ways. When enemies seem to triumph, the imprecatory psalms help us talk to God honestly by reminding us that we can trust the God who is on His throne.

Altar Moments

1. Read Hebrews 10:32–35 and 11:32–38. How do the responses of these believers adjust our focus in our times of suffering?

2. What changes need to be made in your thinking and actions regarding your enemies? How does Paul's response to the Philippian jailer encourage you?

3. How could the imprecatory psalms be helpful to us as we process anger and hurt over mistreatment?

Prayer:

Dear Lord,

"It's good to long for and to work for justice and to live for the day of ultimate justice. But I need and I must heed your warning to avoid a vengeful spirit.... like I would run from coiled rattlesnakes, toxic fumes, or E. coli–poisoned waters. No matter what the provocation.... You are telling me I have no right to revenge, no right to gloat when an enemy falls, no right to get back at or to get even with anybody. I'm so glad you didn't 'get even' with me, Father, for all the ways I rebelled (and do rebel) against you, for all the ways I've chosen my gain over your glory, for all the ways I've misrepresented you to the world, even to my own heart. You didn't get even; you got generous. May the cross of Jesus keep me humble, patient, and expectant of the day of consummate justice. I don't want to waste one more self-absorbed moment relishing personal revenge. There are much better things to eat. I pray in Jesus' merciful and mighty name. Amen."[5]

---

5   Smith, *Everyday Prayers*, location 3362, Kindle edition.

Chapter 13

Altar Living in a Cancel Culture

"Do not be overcome by evil, but overcome evil
with good." Romans 12:21

*E*ARLY IN MY CHRISTIAN life, I was intrigued by the
question asked by D. James Kennedy in his book, *What
If Jesus Had Never Been Born?* Kennedy wrote, "Had He never
come, the hole would be a canyon about the size of a continent.
Christ's influence on the world is immeasurable."[1] Actually, I
think the canyon would be much larger than a continent. In trying to fathom a Christ-less world, I have the mental picture of
the worst dystopian environment imaginable with unspeakable
misery—literally hell on earth.

One of the biggest miscalculations people make is to think
that all we enjoy in this life is provided through human achieve-
ment or chance. Little thought is given to the truth that God
"makes his sun rise on the evil and on the good and sends rain

---

1   D. James Kennedy and Jerry Newcombe, *What If Jesus Had Never Been Born?*
    (Nashville: Thomas Nelson Publishers, 1994), 4.

on the just and on the unjust" (Matt. 5:45). This common grace which should lead us to worship the living God is categorically rejected by this world. Yet, in addition to God's common grace, God's people also receive His redemptive grace found in Christ which results in good works flowing from His redeemed people.

The impact of Christ's life continues to influence millions of people to love and good deeds. Kennedy communicates that point eloquently when he writes, "Many of man's noblest and kindest deeds find their motivation in love for Jesus Christ; and some of our greatest accomplishments also have their origin in service rendered to the humble Carpenter of Nazareth."[2] The teaching and example of Christ have influenced such developments as hospitals, universities, education, government, modern science, respect for women, benevolence, value of human life, compassion ministries, jurisprudence, sexual ethic, work ethic, codification of language, literature, music, and countless changed lives because of the gospel.[3] The power of Jesus Christ continues to transform every aspect of human life as believers seek to do good in His name.

We conclude this section with the all-encompassing command in verse 21. I belabor this a bit only to emphasize this important motivation. Altar Living means that in the blows of life, we are not to be "overcome by evil, but overcome evil with good" (Rom. 12:21). Furthermore, we are to pursue good works even in the face of evil, giving evidence of our faith, so that others may see and glorify our Father in heaven (Matt. 5:16). Three

---

2   Ibid, iii.
3   Ibid, 3–4.

times in Romans 12, Paul references the believer's response to evil—we are to hate evil (v. 9); we are never to repay evil for evil (v. 17); and not to be overcome by evil (v. 21). Considering these truths is important for us who live in a contentious and vindictive world, a world intent on settling scores by revenge and cancellation.

The reason behind this command in verse 21 is likely because of the strong temptation to respond in kind when persecution comes. The path forward is to avoid being entangled in the evil strategies and behaviors of this age. Jesus taught His followers to love their enemies and bear insults from their detractors. His teaching was more than mere words; Jesus modeled what He taught and nowhere more clearly than from the cross where He prayed, "Father, forgive them, for they know not what they do" (Luke 23:34).

Altar Life calls us to emit the aroma of Christ as we live in a hostile world (2 Cor. 2:15–16). Paul similarly urged the Philippians to live "blameless and innocent, children of God without blemish in the midst of a crooked and twisted generation, among whom you shine as lights in the world, holding fast to the word of life" (Phil. 2:15–16).

These warnings and challenges provide important guidance for us to stay focused on Christ when the lines are blurred by painful and perplexing issues. How do we avoid being conquered by evil when the divisions are deep, and the conversations are so charged? How is doing good possible when such efforts are so often maligned and spoken of as evil? These questions come to mind as I think of the church's endeavors to fulfill

God's command to make disciples in the turbulent and hostile waters of our culture.

In thinking through what it means to live for Christ in an antagonistic culture, believers need to consider several points of perspective. First, the history of the church is a road marked by suffering. The church in America has had relatively unprecedented freedom, which has not been the norm for the church throughout the rest of the world. God's people have a track record of advancing the gospel while enduring systematic persecution. Second, in navigating the present hostility to biblical truth, we need to live circumspect lives. Such lives are guided by wisdom, faith, and courage in the present cancel culture (Eph. 5:15–17). If we are to avoid being overcome by evil, we need to redirect our focus while living through the challenges before us. Third, God will always be our "refuge and an ever-present help in a time of trouble" (Psa. 46:1). He remains the supreme sovereign of the universe and delights when His people call out to Him for help. The cause is His, and yet, in the culture wars of recent years, believers have tended to be more engaged in political maneuvering than in seeking God's help. May we seek Him for help first and above all.

The Road Marked by Suffering

Presenting ourselves to God means our lives bear a resemblance to Christ. We have referred to such a life in Part 3 as "supernatural living." How else would we describe the giving of ourselves for others, doing good to our enemies, or blessing our persecutors? We are called to live this way despite a world that is hostile to Christ.

The ministry of the first disciples, as well as that of committed believers through the centuries, bear witness to the sober promises of suffering given by Jesus. John Foxe chronicled the persecution of early Christians in his classic work, *Foxe's Christian Martyrs of the World*. Foxe begins with Jesus Christ, and then goes to Stephen, the first martyr (Acts 7), followed by the disciples:

- James, the son of Zebedee, was beheaded at the request of Herod Agrippa.
- Philip was thrown in prison, scourged, and afterward crucified by his persecutors.
- Matthew was killed with the sword.
- Mark was seized, his feet tied together, and he was dragged through the streets and left bruised and bleeding in a dungeon all night. The next day they burned his body.
- Andrew hung upon a cross for three days, suffering dreadful pain, but continuing constantly to tell the people around him of the love of Jesus Christ.
- Peter, after a nine-month imprisonment, was brought out for execution, and after being scourged, he was crucified with his head downwards. Tradition says that he chose this painful posture because he did not think he was worthy to suffer in the same manner as the Lord.
- Paul was beheaded by Nero.
- Jude was crucified.
- Bartholomew was beaten with clubs.
- Thomas died when a spear was thrust through him.[4]

---

4   John Foxe, *Foxe's Christian Martyrs of the World* (Westwood, NJ: Barbour and Company, Inc., 1985), 11–34.

It is hard for many of us to relate to what the first Christians suffered, and we seem oblivious to the plight of our brothers and sisters who presently suffer under brutal regimes. Every part of their lives is disrupted by persecution. The writer of Hebrews allows us to peek into the first-century experience of believers who were exposed to "reproach and affliction" (Heb. 10:33). When persecution came, they "joyfully accepted the plundering of their property" (v. 34). Only complete surrender to Christ and the promised power of God can produce such a response in the face of crushing blows.

I once met with a house church in East Asia whose pastor had been taken by the police. His family and church lived for weeks not knowing where he was or what had happened. Such an experience is common under their present government where there are no "Miranda Rights" or due process. As I met with this house church, I remember seeing the strain of worry on his wife's face as she wondered if she would ever see him again. This fellowship of believers met in a humble living room. As they sang praises to God and offered prayer on behalf of their pastor, I sensed from their expressions that their burdens were rolled over to the Savior they loved. It was one of the greatest worship experiences I have ever had. I received word after returning home that this faithful pastor was released after weeks of being in jail. His crime? He dared to pastor a local church. This is their status quo.

I'm indebted to ministries like Voice of the Martyrs who exist to tell the stories of the global suffering of our brothers and sisters. We are naturally conditioned to forget global persecution. We don't want to think about believers in East Asia who have lighted cigarettes snuffed out in their nostrils. We have no concept of the pressure they face, as they gather under threat of arrest. We have little comprehension of the intimidation they experience or the financial hardship that comes because they follow Christ. The loss of family relationships and many other deep sorrows are not pressing issues for us, and consequently, we give little thought to them. However, that is changing quickly for the church in the West. The winds of persecution are blowing in our once tranquil land of religious liberty.

Circumspect and Courageous in a Cancel Culture

What does Altar Life look like in the changing scene of American culture? We are seeing the erosion of liberties that have been the foundation of our nation. History is being rewritten with great rapidity. Common values are being jettisoned for the new dogma of the cancel culture.

In his insightful book, *We Will Not Be Silenced*, Erwin Lutzer explains cancel culture this way: "It says yes, you have the First Amendment. You can exercise your freedom of speech. But if you do, we will make sure that you are fired. You will be vilified and ostracized. Cancelled."[5] This new standard of "righteousness" has prevailed in the most powerful institutions of western culture—government, education, entertainment, sports, media, and business. The radical left and social progressives exclude no one from their penetrating gaze, and with the impeccable

---

5   Erwin Lutzer, *We Will Not Be Silenced* (Eugene, OR: Harvest House Publishers, 2020), 105.

memory of the Internet no comment or behavior goes unnoticed or is ever forgotten.

The cancel culture movement devours even their own who deviate from their prescribed narrative and agenda. Bari Weiss, who worked for *The New York Times* as an op-ed staff editor and writer about culture and politics from 2017–2020, is an example of the increasing body count from the radical left. Weiss, hardly an advocate for Christianity or a biblical worldview, resigned from *The Times*, because she was bullied by colleagues for daring to veer from the cancel narrative. Weiss wrote in her resignation letter, "What rules that remain at *The Times* are applied with extreme selectivity. If a person's ideology is in keeping with the new orthodoxy, they and their work remain unscrutinized. Everyone else lives in fear.... Online venom is excused so long as it is directed at the proper targets."[6]

Albert Mohler expressed the stakes of this cultural moment by using an example of biblical marriage: "There will be no place to hide, and there will be no way to remain silent....The question is whether evangelicals will remain true to the teachings of Scripture and the unbroken teaching of the Christian church for over two thousand years on the morality of same-sex acts and the institution of marriage."[7] The sheer force of this moment clamors for conformity, and if you don't conform, you are fired,

---

6 Bari Weiss, "Resignation Letter," accessed September 20, 2021, https://www.bariweiss.com/resignation-letter.

7 Albert Mohler, "God, the Gospel, and the Gay Challenge—A Response to Matthew Vines," accessed August 1, 2021, https://albertmohler.com/2014/04/22/god-the-gospel-and-the-gay-challenge-a-response-to-matthew-vines.

severely penalized, or cancelled from any place at the table of influence.

This certainly is not a new question. Believers have been dealing with this dilemma from the beginning. I'm reminded of the Hebrew midwives in Exodus 2 who were told by the regime of their day to throw all the Hebrew baby boys into the Nile River. Or Shadrach, Meshach, and Abednego who were told to bow to the king's statue or face being thrown into the fiery furnace (Dan. 3). Or the apostles who were told to stop preaching by the religious establishment (Acts 4:18). The kingdom of God and the kingdom of this world have always been in conflict. Lutzer was correct in his assessment: "The day of the casual Christian is over. No longer is it possible to drift along, hoping that no tough choices will have to be made."[8]

In Rod Dreher's book, *Live Not by Lies*, he interviews those who lived under oppressive regimes.[9] Dreher identified the common reaction of those who lived under such conditions who are presently watching the cultural shifts in American life:

> What unnerves those who lived under Soviet communism is this similarity: Elites and elite institutions are abandoning old-fashioned liberalism, based in defending the rights of the individual, and replacing it with a progressive creed that regards justice in terms of groups. It encourages people to identify with groups—ethnic, sexual,

---

8   Erwin Lutzer, *Where Do We Go from Here? Hope and Direction in Our Present Crisis* (Chicago: Moody, 2013), 39.

9   Dreher's title was influenced by an essay with the same title written by Aleksandr Solzhenitsyn in 1974. Solzhenitsyn lived in the former Soviet Union and experienced firsthand the persecution of a totalitarian state.

and otherwise—and to think of Good and Evil as a matter of power dynamics among the groups. A utopian vision drives these progressives, one that compels them to seek to rewrite history and reinvent language to reflect their ideals of social justice.[10]

Dreher's diagnosis describes the forces which want to cancel all things from the past. They argue that every aspect of America's history is rotten from root to stem. Lutzer elaborates on this grand vision of the radical left:

> On the rubble of America's Judeo-Christian past a new America will emerge, which they say will be free of poverty, racism, and white supremacy. The secular left's goal is a future in which everyone will be equal on their terms and the disparities of the past will be read about only in history books. Those who resist this utopian vision are to be vilified, bullied, and shamed until they admit to the mistakes of the past and embrace the secular left's great hope for the future.[11]

In this political landscape, Christians are called to contend earnestly for biblical truth, and we have a moral responsibility to participate in the democratic process. This involvement is part of a biblical witness in the forging of policies and law. However, recent cultural trends weaken public discourse by silencing a biblical worldview. In his insightful work *The Benedict Option*, Rod Dreher describes the present confusion in American culture as, "a civilization in which no one [feels] an obligation to

---

10 Rod Dreher, *Live Not by Lies* (New York: Sentinel, 2020), x–xi, Kindle edition.
11 Lutzer, *We Will Not Be Silenced*, 19.

the past, to the future, to each other, or to anything higher than self-gratification,"[12] and because of this loss of identity, we are a nation that "is dangerously fragile."[13]

As I take this diversion to look at cultural developments in the United States, I'm not arguing that the history of our country is perfect. On the contrary, our nation is stained by many grievous acts and policies. Nevertheless, the United States has been a place of refuge for millions of people searching for freedom, new beginnings, and hope for a better life. Presently, legal standing is provided for every citizen to pursue their personal goals. However, today, many are driven by rage to dismantle our national way of life in a misguided pursuit of justice.

Again, Dreher's analysis is solid, especially his emphasis on the spiritual dynamics of the situation:

> The Western world has become post-Christian, with large numbers of those born after 1980 rejecting religious faith. This means that they will not only oppose Christians when we stand up for our principles—in particular, in defense of the traditional family, of male and female gender roles, and of the sanctity of human life—but also they will not even understand why they should tolerate dissent based in religious belief. We cannot hope to resist the coming soft totalitarianism if we do not have our spiritual lives in order.[14]

---

12 Rod Dreher, *The Benedict Option: A Strategy for Christians in a Post-Christian Nation* (New York: Sentinel, Penguin Random House, 2017), 89–90.

13 Ibid, 90.

14 Dreher, *Live Not by Lies*, xii–xiii.

The church has made the mistake of waging these battles solely through the political process. Yes, we can influence legislation and contend for good policy. Yet, this is a spiritual struggle, and we would do well to remember that "though we walk in the flesh, we do not wage war according to the flesh. For the weapons of our warfare are not of the flesh but have divine power to destroy strongholds" (2 Cor. 10:3–4). How are we to live in this present spiritual conflict?

We Are People of the Truth

Aleksandr Solzhenitsyn was arrested in his native Russia (Soviet Union) on February 12, 1974. On that same day he released his essay "Live Not by Lies." Within 24 hours he was exiled to the United States where he was received with a warm welcome. His parting words to his countrymen urged them to recognize the power of individuals refusing to cooperate with the lies of the regime. Solzhenitsyn's charge is wise counsel and provides insight on how to overcome evil with good. As followers of Christ, we are to be men and women of integrity who stand on revealed truth. When the apostles were told to stop preaching in Jerusalem, they responded by saying, "Whether it is right in the sight of God to listen to you rather than to God, you must judge, for we cannot but speak of what we have seen and heard" (Acts 4:19–20). What does it mean to be a people of the truth in a culture of deception? It means that:

- If the prevailing opinions and attitudes declare, "There is no God!" We must insist that God is true and everyone is a liar (Rom. 3:4), for God's Word declares that we are created in His image and before Him "we live and move and have our being" (Acts 17:28).

- If the majority opinion says it is permissible to kill a baby in the womb and provides a legal right to do so, we are compelled to say, "God has commanded, 'You shall not murder'" (Exod. 20:13). The Lord God has formed our inward parts and knitted each of us together in our mother's womb. Indeed, we are fearfully and wonderfully made" (Psa. 139:13–14).

- If the culture divides along racial lines, we must say, "There is no partiality with God. We are all created from one blood; therefore, we should love our neighbor as ourselves and strive for justice in our shared, fallen world. We have come to see that true unity is found in Christ where all believers are one in Him" (Rom. 2:11; Acts 17:27; Gal. 3:28).

- If everyone in the world declares that fornication, adultery, homosexuality, and the agendas that champion these behaviors are good, right, and loving, we must say with no malice, only compassion, "[D]o you not know the unrighteous will not inherit the kingdom of God? Do not be deceived: neither the sexually immoral, nor idolaters, nor adulterers, nor men who practice homosexuality, nor thieves, nor the greedy, nor drunkards, nor revilers, nor swindlers will inherit the kingdom of God" (1 Cor. 6:9–10).

- If the movers and shakers of this world insist that the number of genders is endless or that marriage can be defined in a myriad of ways, then we must say, "God created man in His own image, in the image of God He created him; male and female He created them" (Gen. 1:27). The Lord God defined marriage in the context of creation between a man and a woman, and "a man shall leave his father and his mother and hold fast to his wife, and they shall become one flesh" (2:24).

- If the false prophets of our day declare that there are many ways to God, we must stand on the exclusivity of Christ who stated in simple terms, "I am the way, and the truth, and the life. No one comes to the Father except through me" (John 14:6). We will stand with the apostle Peter who proclaimed, "There is salvation in no one else, for there is no other name under heaven given among men by which we must be saved" (Acts 4:12).

These statements are not declared from an adversarial position toward others but from a heart to obey Christ who is our life (Col. 3:4). Consequently, we refuse to cooperate with the lies in our culture and choose to stand upon God's revealed truth in Scripture. Though none go with us, this is the path we must follow as we live Life on the Altar.

We Are People of Love

Paul encouraged the Ephesians to speak "the truth in love" (Eph. 4:15). In context, he is describing teaching in the church body. God's truth is to be relayed in love for the building up of the church and for our witness to the world. There is a tragic disconnect when biblical truth is communicated in a harsh, legalistic, and unloving way.

Inside the church, believers are to speak the truth in love. The same is true in this hostile world. In Colossians 4, Paul counseled the believers to "walk in wisdom toward outsiders, making the best use of the time. Let your speech always be gracious, seasoned with salt, so that you may know how you ought to answer each person" (vv. 5–6). Navigating the difficult circumstances of the present cultural landscape will require a daily application of these verses. Whether at work, school, athletic events, or in whatever sphere you find yourself as a follower of Christ, we are called to walk circumspect with words that are gracious and truthful. Furthermore, we are called to be thoughtful and prayerful about our witness, even thinking through conversations and potential situations of our day so that we will know how to answer others.

John Stonestreet encourages believers to build a theology of getting fired.[15] Stonestreet is not advocating a reckless approach by any means: he simply urges Christians to think through their witness and examine their conscience to determine their boundaries of compliance in the workplace. This is a call to walk in truth and in love.

We Are People in Community

Church life for the Christian is crucial especially in times of suffering and persecution. While the church in the United States is not presently experiencing systematic persecution, we are seeing what Dreher describes as a "soft totalitarianism."[16] Dreher explains this term as demanding "allegiance to a set of progressive beliefs, many of which are incompatible with logic—and certainly with Christianity. Compliance is forced less by the state

---

15 John Stonestreet and Shane Morris, "Theology of Getting Fired—Ask Break-point." *Breakpoint: Colson Center*, November 18, 2020, https://breakpoint.org/building-a-theology-of-getting-fired-ask-breakpoint/.

16 Dreher, *Live Not by Lies*, xii.

than by elites who form public opinion, and by private corporations that, thanks to technology, control our lives far more than we would like to admit."[17] Dreher's words can be observed with nearly every news cycle.

This is a time for believers to draw near to God and one of the most significant ways we can do that is through faithfully attending a local church. The power of the gathered church inspires confidence in the promises and purposes of God. We need what only church life can provide, namely—worship, instruction, fellowship, and mission/purpose. As we emphasized in chapter 8, forsaking the gathering of God's people is to our own peril and Christ's dishonor.

We Are People Who Hope in the Lord

These times in which we live could be one of the greatest opportunities for the church to shine, as we face this present darkness. Consider the example of King Hezekiah recorded in the Old Testament. While not perfect, Hezekiah did what was right in the eyes of the Lord (2 Chron. 31:20). The circumstances Hezekiah faced, and the way he responded, give insight for this hour.

Several passages of the Old Testament contain the account of Sennacherib's invasion of Judah (2 Chron. 32; 2 Kings 18, 19; and Isa. 36, 37). Sennacherib, the king of Assyria, had sacked the northern tribes of Israel leaving a tremendous wake of destruction and despair in his path and was a clear and present danger to Hezekiah and the southern kingdom of Judah.

---

17 Ibid, 7.

In Isaiah 36, Sennacherib focused his military might on the fortified cities of Judah. He sent the Rabshakeh, an important official in the Assyrian military, to deliver a message of sheer intimidation. The Rabshakeh's menacing message was especially effective, because he spoke flawless Hebrew. The people of Judah assembled on the wall and could hear the bullying firsthand. Listen to some of the threats unleashed upon Hezekiah and the people of Judah:

- He mocked their faith, "On what do you rest this trust of yours?" (Isa. 36:4).
- He scoffed at their weakness by saying that even if Assyria gave Judah two thousand horses (if Judah were able to set riders on them) … a single captain among the least of Assyria could defeat Judah (vv. 8–10).
- The Rabshakeh introduced confusion by claiming that the Lord had told Assyria to destroy Judah (v. 10).
- Speaking in their language, and in the hearing of many, the Rabshakeh said, "You are doomed to eat your own dung and drink your own urine" (Isa. 36:12). Yes, that's in the Bible!
- The Rabshakeh attacked the leadership of Hezekiah by saying, "Do not let Hezekiah deceive you…. Do not let Hezekiah make you trust in the Lord…. Make your peace with me and come out to me" (vv. 14,16).

This was a full-frontal attack on the minds and hearts of God's people. Yet, this account is a demonstration of how the people of God should respond when fear and intimidation come.

First, the people of God were silent. They were not driven by their emotions, including fear, neither did they default to unbelief. This seems like a contradiction, where we are not to be silent in speaking the truth. But their silence under these circumstances was confidence, not cowardice. Isaiah 36:21 reads, "They were silent and answered him not a word, for the king's command was, 'Do not answer him.'" When bad news comes, when we are assaulted by threats and intimidation, to whom do we listen? This event in the Old Testament reminds us to be still and remember who is on the throne.

Second, Hezekiah and Judah's leaders sought the Lord. Their silence was not a mere stoicism; they refused to answer the Rabshakeh in kind. Rather, they sought with desperation and determination the God of heaven. Hezekiah "tore his clothes and covered himself with sackcloth and went into the house of the LORD" (Isa. 37:1).

Third, Hezekiah stood strong on the promises of God. Isaiah spoke an assuring word, "Do not be afraid because of the words that you heard … Behold, I will make him fall by the sword in his own land" (Isa. 37:6–7). Likewise, in our trials, we can stand on God's promise that we will never be abandoned and that our lives are in His hands (Heb. 13:5).

A final observation from this text is that our battles are the Lord's. Hezekiah had sought the Lord in prayer and was told by Isaiah, "Because you have prayed to me concerning Sennacherib … I will defend this city to save it, for my own sake and for the sake of my servant David" (Isa. 37:21, 35). One of the greatest demonstrations of God's power in the Old Testament followed. The siege of Jerusalem was broken when the angel of the Lord killed 185,000 Assyrians in a single night (2 Kgs.

19:35). Sennacherib withdrew and returned to Nineveh in Assyria, where his own sons killed him.

When the Rabshakehs of this world launch their vile threats, remember that God delights to show His power and glory, so let us stand resolved with the psalmist who said, "When I am afraid, I put my trust in You" (Psa. 56:3). May we never be overcome with evil but may the grace of our Savior be on display for all to see.

Altar Moments

1. Have you thought about a world in which Christ never came? What would that world be like? What motivates you to do good works in Christ's name?

2. Because of the danger of advocating "good works/deeds" as a way to salvation, we often minimize our calling to pursue good works in living out our faith. Read the book of Titus in the New Testament and identify how many times the word "good" and "good works" are referenced for the believer. Can you list five good works that should be pursued in the Christian life?

3. What is evil? What are ways that you are vulnerable to being overcome by evil? How does it help you to think and act on overcoming evil by doing good?

4. What are some present challenges that you face that are in opposition to your faith in Christ? How does the example in

Daniel 6 encourage us as we walk in wisdom in an unbelieving culture?

Prayer:

"O my Lord, life in the gospel follows the way of the cross. It entails conflict. Inevitably, it must, not because I want it so but because the world I live in has surrendered to your enemy and embraced his demonic values. I am often opposed, Lord.... But you understand my anguish, for you yourself endured suffering at the hands of evil men. And you did not retaliate....

And yet you won, for you stuck to what was right and kept entrusting your case to God.... I would rather lose with you, dear Lord, than win with the world.... Let me lose now, if I have to, so that I may hear your 'Well Done' then. In your holy name, Amen."[18]

---

18 Raymond C. Ortlund, Jr. *A Passion for God: Prayers and Meditations on the Book of Romans* (Wheaton: Crossway Books, 1994), 170–71.

Part 4

Presenting Ourselves to God for the Advance of the Gospel

LTAR LIFE IS FOCUSED on the spread of the gospel. In Part 4, our attention shifts to the theme of advancing the gospel found in Romans 12–16. The spread of the gospel was the dominant theme as the apostle Paul concluded his letter to the Romans. Paul sought to guide this church to support the missionary efforts under the banner of the gospel. This should be the agenda of every church.

Paul had not planted the church in Rome himself and was a bit of an outsider to this congregation. By the time of Paul's writing, the church had already existed for some time and was made up of both Jews and Gentiles. The cultural differences abounded and are referenced as a common struggle in the New Testament (Acts 15). Because of these developments, the church at Rome faced significant factions and schisms. The church had issues to resolve and would need grace to work through these differences.

Paul appeals for unity throughout the closing chapters of Romans. As mentioned earlier, nearly one-third of the "one another" commands in the New Testament are found in Romans 12–16. These "one another" commands are aimed at unity within the body as Paul charges them not to "pass judgment on one another any longer" (Rom. 14:13). Furthermore, he calls them to "accept one another" (Rom. 15:7), "admonish one another" (Rom. 15:14), and "greet one another with a holy kiss" (Rom. 16:16). Each of these directives is given in order to foster genuine Christian love among this church family. This application of the gospel is a timeless guide for every local church. This challenge should impact the body of Christ as we seek unity in the gospel for obedience to the Great Commission.

Chapter 14 will concentrate on Paul's missionary vision for taking the message of Christ to the ends of the earth. Paul's ministry goal is consistent with two foundational texts Jesus gave to His disciples as parting commands, Matthew 28:18–20 and Acts 1:8. These verses are commonly referred to as "The Great Commission" and were given as a final charge from Jesus to His disciples. This chapter will look at Paul's focus on gospel advancement through his relationship with the church at Rome, challenging us to view the world through the concentric circles of Acts 1:8.

Chapter 15 emphasizes the importance of doctrinal unity in healthy ministry to our neighborhoods as well as to the nations. In this chapter, we consider the church in Antioch in Acts 11. This congregation is a wonderful example of the harmony and spiritual fervor we should seek. We will also consider doctrinal commitments important to gospel partnerships.

Chapter 16 will close our journey with a glimpse of our future in Christ. Life on the Altar leads to fellowship with God as we commune with Him in the fellowship of salvation. It culminates in His very presence when our faith becomes sight. We will conclude with the thrill of what it means to be destined for heaven. The gathering of the redeemed in Christ is far from being haphazard or thrown together as history seems to careen out-of-control. It is the plan of God from the foundation of the world.

Chapter 14

Viewing the World through an Acts 1:8 Concentric

"Finally, brothers, pray for us, that the word of
the Lord may speed ahead and be honored."
2 Thessalonians 3:1

S. D. GORDON ONCE WROTE of an imagined conversation in heaven between the ascended Jesus and the angel
Gabriel. In this fictitious conversation, Jesus and Gabriel are
talking intently about Christ's completed earthly journey.

Gabriel said, "Master, You died for sinners down
there, didn't You?"

Jesus answered Gabriel in the affirmative.

"You must have suffered greatly," Gabriel continued.

"Yes," Jesus responded.

"And does all the world know about it?" Gabriel wondered.

Jesus said, "Only a few in Palestine know about it so far."

Gabriel was uneasy and probed, "Master, what is Your plan? What have You done to ensure that the world will know of Your saving work?"

"Well," Jesus said, "I asked Peter, James, and John, and some others down there to make it the purpose of their lives to tell others, and the others are instructed to tell others, and the others are to tell others, and yet others, and still others, until the last person in the farthest circle has heard the Good News of my redeeming work through my life, death, and resurrection."[1]

This didn't seem like a good plan to Gabriel. After all, he had been dispatched from heaven to earth on many occasions, and this trusted angel was fully aware of human frailty and failure. Gabriel hesitated awkwardly, and then pressed Jesus,

"Yes, Lord but suppose that Peter fails. What if John simply doesn't follow through and tell others. What if they are overcome by distractions or despair? And what if they just don't do it? What other plans have You made?" Jesus' quiet, wondrous voice said to His trusted messenger, "Gabriel, I haven't made any other plans."[2]

---

1   Adapted from S. D. Gordon and Samuel Dickey, *Quiet Talks: The Complete Collection* (A public domain book), location 11483, Kindle edition.
2   Ibid.

Jesus' plan for taking His redeeming work to the nations was through the feeble and frail efforts of His disciples. God's sovereign power was on display as this ragtag band of disciples went forth in Holy Spirit power declaring the excellencies of Christ to anyone who would hear. This first wave of gospel impact began in Jerusalem at Pentecost (Luke 2). By the end of Paul's ministry, the message had reached Rome and was advancing toward Spain and beyond. The commission of the church has not changed.

Gospel advance is one of the themes in Romans, a letter Paul began by declaring, "I am not ashamed of the gospel, for it is the power of God for salvation to everyone who believes" (Rom. 1:16). His life was given to this mission, and on one occasion Paul wrote, "Woe to me if I do not preach the gospel" (1 Cor. 9:16). This mindset should grip the church and be uppermost in the heart of every believer. This is precisely how Jesus Christ commanded His people to live.

Two passages express Christ's commission in clear terms. Matthew's Gospel closes with the post-resurrection command of Christ to His disciples: "Go therefore and make disciples of all nations, baptizing them in the name of the Father and of the Son and of the Holy Spirit, teaching them to observe all that I have commanded you. And behold, I am with you always, to the end of the age" (Matt. 28:19–20). This message given to the disciples and to the church is God's plan for the ages. We are reading this page because the first disciples, and those who believed on their message, were obedient to this charge.

A second text containing Christ's commission is Acts 1:8 which was given by Jesus in the forty days between His resurrection and ascension. This text captures the mission of the church as Jesus spoke, "But you will receive power when the Holy Spirit has come upon you, and you will be my witnesses in Jerusalem and in all Judea and Samaria, and to the end of the earth." The book of Acts fills in the storyline of the gospel spreading in concentric circles beginning in Jerusalem, Judea, Samaria, and throughout the Roman Empire. It has been suggested that the book of Acts could be summarized as the Savior went up, the Spirit came down, and the church went out.

Interestingly, the last verse in the book of Acts ends with an adverb translated as "without hindrance" (Acts 28:31), referring to the unhindered spread of the gospel. Indeed, Paul witnessed the gospel triumph over many barriers, and it remained unhindered even though he was under house arrest. The Christian faith is founded upon the success of the gospel; rebel hearts are conquered by the transforming power of Jesus Christ. This is a never-ending story as every new generation of believers is called to advance the gospel through a surrendered life.

Recapturing an Acts 1:8 View of the World

We need to recapture what it means to view the world as Jesus outlined in Acts 1:8. This does not come easily for us. We typically forget those outside of our immediate sight. Some years back, Paul Borthwick illustrated this point in his book. *Six Dangerous Questions to Transform Your View of the World*. Borthwick referenced a National Geographic advertisement which stated that "24 million Americans can't find our country on a map of the world."[3] Borthwick continued, "As a follower of Jesus Christ, I find that geographic knowledge follows my beliefs. My Christian commitment demands that I be concerned about the world for which Jesus died. Yet I find that quite a few Christians are no different from the population surveyed for … the National Geographic Society."[4] Yes, we all have local commitments where we spend the preponderance of our time and energy. Yet, we can be so fixated on ourselves and maintaining of our "Jerusalem" ministries that we forget about the sea of lostness that fills this world.

To this point, one of the joys of the Christian life is living where our commitments intersect with the truth of the biblical text. This is particularly true when it comes to obedience to Christ's command to be a witness for the gospel. With such a clear mandate, why do believers and churches often seem to slumber in a time of great need? Vance Havner was credited with saying, "The tragedy of our times is that the situation is desperate, but the saints are not." We are plagued by misplaced priorities and menacing distractions.

Killing Rats and the Kingdom of God

Charles Spurgeon tells a story from his youth that speaks to the priorities in a believer's life. On one occasion his grandmother promised him a penny for every hymn of Isaac Watts that he

---

3 Paul Borthwick, *Six Dangerous Questions to Transform Your View of the World* (Downers Grove, IL: InterVarsity Press, 1996), 9. In recent years, national assessment tests have revealed that little has changed since the National Geographic advertisement in 1996.

4 Ibid.

could perfectly repeat to her. Possessing a photographic memory, he began to quickly learn the hymns at such a pace that she reduced the price to a half-penny and eventually to a quarter-penny. Spurgeon recalled that even with the reduction in price there was still risk of her being ruined by his repeated calls on her purse.

In time, Spurgeon faced a lucrative distraction. His grandfather, finding his home overrun with rats, promised Spurgeon a shilling a dozen for all the rats that he could kill. With such an offer, his priorities shifted as he gave up hymn-learning for rat-killing. In later years, Spurgeon confessed that memorizing the hymns paid better: "The hymns have remained with me, while those old rats for years have passed away, and the shillings I earned by killing them have been spent long ago."[5]

Thinking through the cacophony of demands for our time and resources, we are faced with a choice like Spurgeon's. In the Christian life, often the issue is not between good and evil, but between better and best, good and excellent. Who can argue that the eradication of rats is not a good thing when they overrun one's property? But when such activity becomes long term and siphons off our full energy from what is excellent, it becomes a well-disguised distraction that can be justified with palatable excuses.

I sense this was the struggle in Acts 6 over the care of widows. With the rapid expansion of the Jerusalem church following Pentecost, the needs of this young body were great, and the

---

5 Charles H. Spurgeon, *My Autobiography: Charles Haddon Spurgeon* (Public domain, copyright by Simon D. Turner, 2011), location 831, Kindle edition.

apostles were battling the issue of calling. They certainly were not communicating that they were above waiting on tables and meeting physical needs, but their calling was clearly "to prayer and to the ministry of the word" (Acts 6:4).

The evaluation between good and excellent can rarely be made on the fly. Such decisions must be made through regular times of prayer and reflection about the commitments of our lives. The psalmist's prayer goes to the heart of the matter: "So teach us to number our days, that we may present to you a heart of wisdom" (Psa. 90:12). Likewise, the apostle Paul spoke of this tension when he wrote to the Philippians, "And this I pray, that your love may abound still more and more in real knowledge and all discernment, so that you may approve the things that are excellent, in order to be sincere and blameless until the day of Christ" (1:9–11).

An abounding love established in real knowledge and discernment helps us to approve that which is excellent in the Christian life and in the commitments of a local church. We are told in the New Testament that believers "must all appear before the judgment seat of Christ" (2 Cor. 5:10). This reckoning of the redeemed is not concerning salvation, but reward. Paul continues by indicating the purpose, "so that each one may receive what is due for what he has done in the body, whether good or evil" (v. 10). This teaching is to motivate godly living. With that day approaching, we don't want to live our lives engaged in core commitments that have no divine mandate. We don't want to hear our Savior say at the end of our days, "Who told you to pursue that commitment? Why did you devote your heart to that endeavor? Why did you give much of your life to those things that had no eternal value?"

May we approve what is excellent and number our days accordingly. Otherwise, we might commit to lesser priorities and spend our time killing rats and thereby missing what is truly excellent.

Missions Begets Missions

Our church's journey to embrace Acts 1:8 has been a time of discovery. I am amazed how God can use a small and ordinary congregation to make a global impact. Since our first mission trip together in 1998, we have sent out over 60 teams on short-term mission projects. We have rejoiced to see God call out of our congregation men and women, young and old, to champion the gospel in faraway places.

In 2001, we adopted an unreached people group in the Middle East. This was a needed commitment for us as we targeted our prayers and resources on this people group. Praying for a nation that had less than 1% Christian was a sobering exercise for us as a church. We participated stateside in events where immigrants from this country lived. We sent teams to the region and advocated for the spiritual needs of these people, knowing all the while that for those who professed Christ in their country, their lives would be threatened by persecution.

We have also seen God call out of our fellowship those committed to full-time mission service. We have experienced as a congregation the purifying power of missions as our priorities adjusted to mirror Acts 1:8. At the time of this writing, we have ongoing ministry commitments concentrically from South Louisiana to the ends of the world. We are partners with a church plant in New Orleans as well as offering seminary training to pastors in East Asia. We have celebrated many times as our teams have returned with incredible stories of divine appointments and encouraging developments, as God moved across His world drawing men and women to Himself.

When God's people are obedient to the Great Commission, doors are opened for meaningful partnerships in ministry. From my experience, I can confirm that going on missions seems to beget more missions. The more we expose ourselves to gospel work concentrically, partnerships are forged by the Holy Spirit for a strengthened effort.

Pastors and church leaders don't need to re-invent the wheel regarding mission work. Resources and opportunities are readily available to help your church get started with a global focus. Our first mission trip was by invitation from another church that had a developed ministry in Mexico. We piggy-backed on their work as they imparted valuable how-to information. The following year we led our own trip and have routinely returned for over twenty years. In that time, we have developed new local partners and have experienced mutual encouragement as the gospel has been sown and the church edified. As you consider obedience in your life to Acts 1:8, prayerfully consider going on a mission trip.[6] To quote a well-known commercial, "Just Do It."

---

6   FBCG cooperates with the Southern Baptist Convention network of ministries which include the International Mission Board (IMB – www.imb.org) and the North American Mission Board (NAMB – www.namb.org). These partnerships provide numerous resources for Acts 1:8 connections.

Besides going on a trip, opportunities abound on how to be engaged meaningfully with the Acts 1:8 commission. Whether it is through organizing prayer efforts, hosting international students, adopting an unreached people group, inviting a missionary to your church to share about their work, or developing a missions resource area in your church, there are endless ways to promote the cause of Christ around the world.

Those Who Have Gone before Us

I have found reading missionary biographies to be one of the most enriching experiences of my life. These books help us obey the admonition of Hebrews 13:7, which states, "Remember your leaders, those who spoke to you the Word of God. Consider the outcome of their way of life, and imitate their faith." Every generation must deal with the temptation of forsaking the voices of the past in the arrogance of thinking they are the smartest and greatest generation who has ever lived. Reading of the courage, faith, and resolve of those who have gone before us, challenges such pride and motivates us to give our best for Christ.[7]

William Carey (1761–1834) is considered by many to be the "Father of Modern Missions." Carey's biography is an incredible story of how a cobbler with a burden to obey the Great Commission left an eternal impact. While Carey made and mended shoes, he often looked at a crude map of the world affixed to the

---

7   I commend three biographies that have been especially meaningful to my life and ministry: J. Hudson Taylor, *Hudson Taylor* (Minneapolis: Bethany House Publishers, 1987); Timothy George, *Faithful Witness: The Life and Mission of William Carey* (Birmingham, AL: New Hope, 1991); Edward Judson, *The Life of Adoniram Judson* (New York: Anson D. F. Randolph & Company, 1883).

wall of his workshop. Like the apostle Paul's ambition to take the gospel to Rome and later to Spain, Carey was motivated to leave the stability of his life in England to enter the danger and uncertainty of gospel work among unbelieving peoples.

On May 31, 1792, Carey was given the assignment of preaching to ministers and messengers from 24 associated churches gathered in Nottingham, England. His text was Isaiah 54:2–3: "Enlarge the place of your tent, and let the curtains of your habitations be stretched out; do not hold back; lengthen your cords and strengthen your stakes. For you will spread abroad to the right and to the left, and your offspring will possess the nations." Carey understood Isaiah's words to mean that there is to be an enlargement of God's people, an assembling of others on the right and the left, a winning of unbelievers who are yet to be included in the covenant of grace. The sermon came to a crescendo when he said, "Expect great things; attempt great things."[8]

Carey "was keenly aware of God's sovereignty in awakening the Church from its slumber and sending it forth to accomplish His eternal purpose in bringing the lost to a saving knowledge of the Redeemer."[9] The collective gains of Carey's ministry remain a consistent testimony of how God can take a few loaves and fish and multiply them beyond comprehension.

Planting Yourself for the Glory of Christ

Much has been written on the life and work of Adoniram Judson and rightly so. I came face-to-face with the legacy of Judson

---

8   George, *Faithful Witness*, 32.
9   Ibid.

through the urging of a friend who loaned me the biography written by Judson's son, Edward. I devoured the 600 pages (and footnotes). I was deeply moved by Judson's singular passion to make known the gospel to those with no access to it. He was a gospel-centered missionary who let goods and kindred go for the sake of Christ.

Perhaps the most moving episode for me in all of Judson's life was the letter he wrote to Ann Hasseltine's father asking for her hand in marriage:

> I have now to ask whether you can consent to part with your daughter early next spring, to see her no more in this world? [W]hether you can consent to her departure to a heathen land, and her subjection to the hardships and sufferings of missionary life? … Can you consent to all this, for the sake of Him who left His heavenly home and died for her and for you; for the sake of perishing, immortal souls; for the sake of Zion and the glory of God? Can you consent to all this, in hope of soon meeting your daughter in the world of glory, with a crown of righteousness brightened by the acclamations of praise which shall redound to her Saviour from heathens saved, through her means, from eternal woe and despair?[10]

Who talks like that anymore? Who thinks like that anymore? And I wonder who had more courage—Ann for going or her father for letting her go? What a wake-up call to a slumbering North American Church!

---

10 Judson, *The Life of Adoniram Judson*, 20.

It was just over 200 years ago that Judson and his wife Ann set sail from Salem, Massachusetts, en route to India later arriving in Burma. No doubt, many on the wharf that day thought that their departure would be such a small deposit with little hope of bearing much fruit.

When they left their native New England, Judson was 24 years old, and his young bride Ann was 23. He would labor in Burma (Myanmar) for 38 years until his death at age 61. In that entire time, he would only return home once, and that after 33 years of being away.

From a human perspective, their departure for the hardships of missionary life was a fool's errand. From heaven's perspective, the investment was viewed much differently. Jesus taught that His kingdom was like a mustard seed which is sown in a field, and though smaller than all other seeds, when full grown is larger than garden plants and becomes a tree (Matt. 13:31–32). In this parable, Jesus explained that what may look insignificant to the world may in fact be something of monumental value and impact.

When I think of Life on the Altar, I think of commitments like those of Judson's. His ministry would be a picture of perseverance as six years passed in his work in Burma without seeing a single convert. Add to this massive suffering from the loss of two wives and four children; unspeakable persecution; and at times, despair so deep that he requested all commendations and letters of his missionary acclaim be destroyed.

Judson loved his enemies, and his life was filled with love and good deeds. Perhaps his greatest labor of love was seen in his creation of a grammar system that paved the way for the translation of the Bible into Burmese.

Fast forward with me from Salem, Massachusetts, 200 years ago to Gonzales, Louisiana, in 2011. One evening, Gonzales Baptist Seafarers' Center Director, Sylvester Wilson, made a routine run to the Mississippi River to pick up a group of seafarers in need of a ride to town to purchase personal items, access the internet, and eat a meal.

Among that group of seafarers was the ship's captain who was from Myanmar. This captain shared with Wilson that his wife was a Christian who was converted as a result of the gospel work done by Adoniram Judson. He further explained that because of Judson's sacrifice, the message of Christ came to her family.

Scholarly works confirm this captain's testimony. David Barrett's *World Christian Encyclopedia* noted that the largest Christian force in Burma is the Burma Baptist Convention, which owes its origin to the pioneering work of the Baptist missionary, Adoniram Judson.[11]

Reading about Judson's life in 1998 made a great impact on me personally and stoked a commitment to view the world through the lens of Acts 1:8. I have had opportunity to go on some 30 international mission trips, and I am presently overseeing a theological education initiative not far from Burma. Additionally, we have the privilege of hosting on our church campus the Louisiana Chin Baptist Church of over 100 believers who claim their spiritual descent from Judson.

---

11 David Barrett, ed., *World Christian Encyclopedia* (New York: Oxford University Press, 1982), 202.

Adoniram Judson's life was a mustard seed well sown. Its tree is mighty, and its foliage continues to offer the shade of redemption in Christ among the nations. The ripple effect of Judson's life is still spoken of all over the world, even in a small town in South Louisiana.

Altar Moments

1. How can you align the commitments of your life for greater obedience to Acts 1:8? Would you prayerfully consider going on a mission trip?

2. If you were approached on the street for a spontaneous on-camera interview and you were asked, "Tell us why you are a follower of Jesus and how you came to that commitment in your life," what would you say? Are you able to communicate your conversion? The content of the gospel? Take some time to think through how you would communicate how your life has changed through the power of Jesus Christ.

3. Read Paul's testimonies in the book of Acts—Acts 22:3–21; 26:1–29. What do you learn from hearing about his conversion experience?

Prayer:

Dear Lord,

When I think about obeying Your commission, I realize I am praying to the One who is able:

To establish me according to the gospel and the preaching of Jesus Christ (Rom. 16:25).

To make all grace abound to me, so that always having all sufficiency in everything,

I may have an abundance for every good deed (2 Cor. 9:8).

To do far more abundantly beyond all that I ask or think (Eph. 3:20).

To guard what I have entrusted to You until that day (2 Tim. 1:12).

To save forever those who draw near to God through Christ (Heb. 7:25).

To keep me from stumbling, and to make me stand in the presence of His glory blameless with great joy (Jude 24–25).[12]

I press on in Your promises.

Amen.

---

12 *Daily Light* (Nashville: Thomas Nelson, 2013), 71.

Gospel Unity and the Sending Power of God

"While they were worshiping the Lord and
fasting, the Holy Spirit said, 'Set apart for me
Barnabas and Saul for the work to which I have
called them.' Then after fasting and praying they
laid their hands on them and sent them off."
Acts 13:2–3

*W*E SHOULD NOT BE surprised that Satan is always
sowing seeds of discord among God's people. The evil
one knows that a church derailed from worshiping and wit-
nessing is his greatest triumph. When believers are crippled by
disputes within the church, little energy is given to what Christ
has called us to do. The hindrances of disunity are not always
seen in outward conflict. These are seen and felt when believers
are tepid in their support of one another or suspicious of each
other's motivations. This discord impacts the effectiveness of a
church's ministry. Like driving a car with the emergency brake

activated, we feel the drag and long for the work of Christ to be at full power. Unity often seems elusive, or even impossible.

While unity will always be hard work, it will never be impossible to experience in your church or mine. Consider the encouragement given from Jesus' high priestly prayer recorded in John 17. In the moments prior to His arrest and crucifixion, Jesus prayed to the Father for Himself (vv. 1–5), His disciples (vv. 6–19), and for those who would believe on Him through the spread of the gospel (vv. 20–26). Jesus poured out His heart in prayer for believers He would leave behind. He prayed for the disciples' joy (v. 13) and their holiness (v. 17). He was also praying that they would walk in the truth (v.17) and for their allegiance to His purposes (v. 18). However, of all the things Jesus prayed about, He spent the most time praying for their unity, and the unity of those who would come behind them. Jesus prayed that we would live in such a way that the church would represent the oneness of the Triune God and provide a compelling witness to the world (John 17:20–23). Unity in the gospel is possible because Jesus prayed for the unified efforts of His people.

A second reason to be encouraged about unity in the church is because of the beautiful examples found both in Scripture and in our experiences. Ken Sande has written resources to help believers pursue unity in this world. In his book, *The Peacemaker*, Sande writes, "When Christians learn to be peacemakers, they can turn conflict into an opportunity to strengthen relationships, preserve valuable resources, and make their lives a testimony to the love and power of Christ."[1] Unity in the body of Christ is challenging as we learn to die to ourselves and, in humility, seek reconciliation with other believers for the cause of Christ.

We understand how a world in rebellion against God lives with divisions, hatred, bitterness, and fractures. But it is the ultimate contradiction when the church is embroiled in the same destructive behaviors. When this is the atmosphere within the church, the thought of unity seems like a pipe dream. When Christians are engaged in constant bickering and in-fighting, the church's motivation for gospel-centered ministry is affected. Many who have come through difficult church conflicts wonder how the prayer of Jesus in John 17 can be so far removed from their experience.

The pursuit of unity in the truth is God's calling for His people. We have referenced the early church in Acts 2:42–47. This was an exciting and desperate time in redemptive history. I love Luke's description of the unity in the gathered body. Everyone kept feeling a sense of awe at what God was doing (v. 43). They lived together in one accord.

I mentioned earlier that my pastorate began with a lot of uncertainty. The church had been filled with internal fighting which led to a series of bad business meetings and a tarnished reputation. In the end, the church was fractured, with many leaving to go to other churches or dropping out of church life altogether. Yet, as we began to worship the Lord together through expository preaching, we experienced many seasons of

---

1   Ken Sande, *The Peacemaker: A Biblical Guide to Resolving Personal Conflict, 3rd edition* (Grand Rapids: Baker Publishing Group, 2004), 12, Kindle edition.

refreshing. The Lord's presence and healing came in many powerful ways. We came to see that the Lord loves His church and that every painful experience in the Christian life is a reminder of our need for God's grace. Unity around the gospel is essential to staying on mission.

Paul's focus in the closing chapters of Romans was a major call for unity in the church for gospel advancement. As noted in chapter 8, nearly one-third of the "one another" commands in the New Testament are found in Romans 12–16. These "one another" commands are aimed at unity within the body as Paul charges them not to "pass judgment on one another any longer" (14:13). He calls them to "accept one another" (15:7), "admonish one another" (15:14), and "greet one another with a holy kiss" (16:16). Each of these directives is given to foster genuine love in Christ among this church family.

In Romans 15 Paul revealed his ministry plans and his need for support to complete them. He expressed that his ambition was to preach the gospel where Christ had never been proclaimed (v. 20). Spain was in his sights, and he hoped for support from the church at Rome in this missionary effort (v. 24). This gift was a major concern for Paul as he had collected from Gentile churches an offering for the poor Jewish believers in Jerusalem (Acts 20–22; 1 Cor. 16; 2 Cor. 9:1–5).

This support was intended to encourage unity in the gospel among Jews and Gentiles. I was helped by one commentator who made the following observation, "The Gentile Christians are indebted to the Jewish Christians who first brought them the gospel. This is simply another proof why the Jewish and Gentile

Romans should live in peace with one another.... [Paul's] con-
cluding prayer is that the God of peace be with them all as one
people of God."[2] His appeal for unity in the gospel was so that
God's redemption would come to all the peoples of the world.

Let's consider the beautiful example of unity found in the
church in Antioch. The story of their monumental ministry is
preserved for us in Acts 11. With God's grace true unity is not
a pipe dream; it is God's desire for His people. Paul wanted the
body of believers in Rome to experience this type of oneness
that would, in turn, benefit the spread of the gospel into new
regions.

A Portrait of a Great Church

The believers in Antioch were a healthy body during a crucial
time:

> Now those who were scattered because of the
> persecution that arose over Stephen traveled as far
> as Phoenicia and Cyprus and Antioch, speaking the
> word to no one except Jews. But there were some of
> them, men of Cyprus and Cyrene, who on coming to
> Antioch spoke to the Hellenists also, preaching the
> Lord Jesus. And the hand of the Lord was with them,
> and a great number who believed turned to the Lord.
> The report of this came to the ears of the church in
> Jerusalem, and they sent Barnabas to Antioch. When
> he came and saw the grace of God, he was glad, and
> he exhorted them all to remain faithful to the Lord
> with steadfast purpose, for he was a good man, full

---

2   Curtis Vaughn and Fred Malone, *Romans* (Cape Coral, FL: Founders Press, 2020), 252.

**of the Holy Spirit and of faith. And a great many
people were added to the Lord. So Barnabas went to
Tarsus to look for Saul, and when he had found him,
he brought him to Antioch. For a whole year they met
with the church and taught a great many people. And
in Antioch the disciples were first called Christians.
(Acts 11:19–26)**

In this passage, Luke charted how the gospel spread from Jerusalem, through Judea, into Samaria, and into Syria where Antioch was located. The persecution of Stephen (Acts 7:54–8:3)
thrust the gospel into these new areas. Christianity had been
mostly a Jewish movement, but this would change through the
pivotal role of the church at Antioch.

Some churches are famous for their architecture or their buildings. Some are famous for their pastors or music. The church in
Antioch was famous for its faithfulness to Christ. Every church
should strive for this unity of purpose. Through sound teaching,
this church that was discipled by Paul and Barnabas ended up
sacrificially sending them to the mission field. God's grace was
on display through changed lives and committed ministry.

The legacy of Antioch is recorded for our encouragement
and as an example of how to export local ministry to the nations.
Let's look at six commitments in the Antioch church that made
them a great congregation.

They Were Courageous in Their Obedience

The church in Antioch was birthed out of persecution. Stephen's
martyrdom pushed the Good News out of Jerusalem in fulfillment of what Jesus promised in Acts 1:8. Even as the church

was established, believers continued to face opposition. They were first called "Christians" at Antioch (v. 26). This new name, which meant "little Christs," was likely a term of ridicule and scorn. What was offered in disgust was a supreme compliment for this faithful congregation.

Church history is filled with examples of God moving His people in times of persecution. While an oppressive regime may overwhelm the church for a season, the kingdom of Christ marches onward. God's plan for gospel advance does not spare His people from suffering. The congregation in Antioch was courageous in serving the Lord among unbelievers in the city. They rejected cultural norms as God was bringing Jew and Gentile believers together into one family. They dared to cross ethnic barriers through the grace of the Lord Jesus Christ.

The Grace of God Was on Display

Signs of God's grace should be evident in every church. After all, believers saved by grace through faith in Jesus should reflect the grace that saved them. The text says that Barnabas "saw" the grace of God when he arrived in Antioch (Acts 11:23). He saw many new believers who had been delivered from idolatry and pagan practices now worshiping and serving the Lord Jesus Christ. We read in this passage that "a great number" (v. 21), and "a great many people" (v. 24) were added to the Lord.

However, the greatest expression of God's grace for Barnabas was when he saw Jew and Gentile sitting at the same table and worshiping in the same congregation. We can only imagine the impression that was made on Barnabas. This was likely the first time Barnabas experienced this unity, and it was all because of the gospel. I imagine Barnabas thinking to himself as he took in this experience, "Only Jesus Christ can do a work like this." Shouldn't that be our desire? Shouldn't we long to be a part of a church whose only explanation for its success is that God brought this ministry together for His glory?

The destruction of racial and cultural barriers was also seen in the leadership in Antioch. Acts 13 mentions a diverse leadership team of both Jews and Gentiles: "Now there were in the church at Antioch prophets and teachers, Barnabas, Simeon who was called Niger, Lucius of Cyrene, Manaen a lifelong friend of Herod the tetrarch, and Saul" (Acts 13:1). These spiritually gifted leaders were from radically different backgrounds. Through the power of the gospel, they were in place at a pivotal moment in the history of the church.

They Were Faithful Using Their Spiritual Gifts

The church in Antioch used their spiritual gifts faithfully in service to Christ. In Chapter 9, we identified how God gives spiritual gifts to every believer to be used for the building up of the church. One of the clear distinctives of the church in Antioch was their heart to serve and to use their gifts.

If we include Barnabas and Paul in the church, we can identify the following spiritual gifts: encouragement (11:23); exhortation and evangelism (vv. 21, 23); faith (vv. 24, 26); teaching (v. 26); prophecy (13:1); giving (13:1–3); and I suspect many others. However, possessing spiritual gifts doesn't matter unless they are being used. This was not a church that sat on their hands or twiddled their thumbs. They were alive to the things of God. There was urgency to their service, and their lives were surrendered to Christ.

Before leaving this point on spiritual gifts, I would like to highlight Barnabas' role in exhorting and encouraging the church. The text says, "He was a good man, full of the Holy Spirit and of faith" (Acts 11:24). We are first introduced to Barnabas in Acts 4. His real name was "Joseph," and his presence in the early church was so magnanimous that the apostles called him "Barnabas" which meant "son of encouragement" (Acts 4:36).

The church faced many needs in her infancy. To meet these needs, Barnabas sold a piece of property and laid the proceeds of the sale at the feet of the disciples (Acts 4:37). He gave sacrificially. He preached faithfully. He invested selflessly. He encouraged generously. What a blessing to the church! May each of us consider how God has gifted us and minister with such a focused, eternal perspective.

They Were Established in Sound Doctrine

The unity we are talking about in this chapter is anchored in the truth of God's Word. Paul described that unity in this way, "Have this mind among yourselves, which is yours in Christ Jesus" (Phil. 2:5). In church life and mission, we are to be of the same mind in Christ. We are to be one-souled in desire and passion as revealed in Scripture.

The church in Antioch was unified in the truth. Barnabas and Paul taught "a great many people" in Antioch (Acts 11:26).

Their teaching established the church for gospel advance. John Piper explains the importance of sound doctrine in communicating the gospel:

> Gospel doctrine matters because the good news is so full and rich and wonderful that it must be opened like a treasure chest, and all its treasures brought out for the enjoyment of the world. Doctrine is the description of these treasures. Doctrine describes their true value and why they are so valuable. Doctrine guards the diamonds of the gospel from being discarded as mere crystals. Doctrine protects the treasures of the gospel from the pirates who don't like the diamonds but who make their living trading them for other stones. Doctrine polishes the old gems buried at the bottom of the chest. It puts the jewels of gospel truth in order on the scarlet tapestry of history so each is seen in its most beautiful place.[3]

Sadly, many Christians seem to be allergic to doctrine and balk at having to think or study about doctrinal truths. This is the ultimate in misplaced priorities. A man once said to me, "Pastor, all I need is John 3:16. I don't need to get bogged down in any other doctrine than that simple message." I said to him, "Really? Well, there is no doubt that John 3:16 is a glorious sum of the gospel, but if John 3:16 is all we need to know, then that is all God would have given to us." But He has given so much more.

---

3   John Piper, *God Is the Gospel: Meditations on God's Love as the Gift of Himself* (Wheaton: Crossway Books, 2005), 22.

John 3:16 is a simple and profound statement of God's saving action to a lost world: "For God so loved the world, that he gave his only Son, that whoever believes in him should not perish but have eternal life." Have you considered the doctrines expressed in this one verse? Just in passing, John 3:16 leads us to the doctrines of God, the Trinity, sin, humanity, salvation, grace, faith, hell, and eternal life. Breaking these teachings down further, we discover the diamonds and gems Piper referred to above.

Jesus taught that the greatest commandment is to love God with all our heart, soul, and mind. It is impossible to fulfill that command without thinking deeply about the other truths also revealed in God's Word. Sound doctrine guides the life of the church and is critical to our walk with Christ as a safeguard to fuel our gospel efforts.[4] For an entire year, Barnabas and Paul worked to establish a solid foundation through their faithful biblical teaching among the believers in Antioch. That foundation prepared the church to engage in one of the most strategic missionary endeavors in the history of the church. More about that endeavor in a moment.

They Were Empowered by the Holy Spirit

The book of Acts records how the Holy Spirit empowered the early church. The church in Antioch is part of that record. In Acts 11:21, this supernatural power is described in this way: "And the hand of the Lord was with them." I love that phrase

---

4   I commend the work by Chris Bruno and Matt Dirks entitled *Churches Partnering Together: Biblical Strategies for Fellowship, Evangelism, and Compassion* (Wheaton: Crossway Books, 2014). This book is written for smaller churches in mind on how to forge effective partnerships in the gospel.

and how it expresses God's presence and guidance in response to their obedience to Him. This anthropomorphism, giving human characteristics to God to express His work, is used throughout the Bible to communicate God's favor or lack thereof.

When the hand of the Lord was against someone or something, it was doomed to failure. When Pharaoh sought to keep the Israelites in bondage, the hand of the Lord was against him. A series of plagues followed, ultimately leading to Israel's redemption from Egypt (Exod. 9:3).

After their deliverance, Moses proclaimed to Israel, "And it shall be to you as a sign on your hand and as a memorial between your eyes, that the law of the LORD may be in your mouth. For with a strong hand the LORD has brought you out of Egypt" (Exod. 13:9).

When the Philistines were in possession of the Ark of the Covenant, they discovered how severe the hand of the Lord could be: "The hand of the LORD was heavy against the people … and he terrified and afflicted them with tumors" (1 Sam. 5:6).

In contrast, we discover in Scripture the comfort of the Lord's hand upon His people as they walk by faith and in obedience to His Word. Joshua called Israel to assemble stones of remembrance when they crossed the Jordan river into the promised land. This monument was to communicate to all the nations of the earth "that the hand of the LORD is mighty, [and] that you may fear the LORD your God forever" (Josh. 4:24).

As we have already noted, "the hand of the Lord" is not confined to the Old Testament. It is used to describe God's empowerment among the church in Antioch. This band of believers was strengthened daily by God's grace found in Christ Jesus. Their ministry was empowered by the Holy Spirit which made them fruitful. Every church can be assured that the hand of the Lord is upon their efforts as their ministry aligns with the Word of God.

They Were Fervent in Seeking the Lord

One final observation about the church in Antioch is that they were fervent in seeking the Lord. The beautiful mingling of doctrinal conviction, obedience to God's Word, and intense passion to seek the Lord through prayer and fasting made them a powerful kingdom asset.[5] God's grace visited this church again and again.

Acts 13:2–3 describes one of the most eventful worship gatherings in the history of Christianity: "While they were worshiping the Lord and fasting, the Holy Spirit said, 'Set apart for me Barnabas and Saul for the work to which I have called them.' Then after fasting and praying they laid their hands on them and sent them off."

As the church sought the Lord together, the text states that the Holy Spirit spoke (v. 2). I don't know exactly how He revealed the message, but the Holy Spirit made clear to the church that they were to send out Barnabas and Saul for the work of sowing the gospel and planting churches. These beloved brothers were

---

5   Fasting is going without food or water for the purpose of seeking God. The spiritual discipline of fasting is mentioned throughout Scripture as a way God's people have sought Him through the ages. Moses, Elijah, Esther, David, Daniel, Ezra, Nehemiah, Jesus, the early church, and the apostle Paul fasted as an expression of humility before the Lord.

gifted and called to this work, and the church in obedience sent them.

These verses are vital to understanding gospel advance. First, the church is to be a mission-sending family. As Jesus sent the disciples out, so God calls out of the church both men and women to proclaim the gospel far and wide. The church in Antioch was sensitive to the Spirit's work among them. Their ministry was driven by a longing to be used by God, and they would be given the privilege of seeing God perform incredible works.

A second takeaway is seen in how the church sent their best to the mission field. You can understand the temptation to be selfish here. What church member in their right mind would send Paul and Barnabas away from the church? I can imagine the potential push back, can't you? "Oh no, we need these gifted brothers to stay so we can be fed. We need them to keep the ministry strong at home." However, this is not the way they acted. In obedience to the Holy Spirit, they sent their most gifted teachers to the nations.

A third observation is the willingness of the local church to provide prayer, support, and accountability for those they sent. Not only did the church send Paul and Barnabas, but they would remain connected for the coming years. This in turn allowed the church to participate in the success of the gospel. Paul and Barnabas would return to Antioch in the coming years to give reports of their ministry efforts (Acts 14:26; 15:22, 30, 35; 18:22).

A final observation is the importance of prayer before going and doing. The book of Acts weaves the prayers of God's people with the demonstrations of God's power. Beginning in Acts 2, the disciples and others were praying in obedience to Christ and in anticipation of the Holy Spirit's coming at Pentecost. When persecution came as they preached Christ in Jerusalem, they prayed for boldness, and the building shook as they offered their requests (Acts 4:23–31). When Peter was imprisoned, the church prayed for his release which was granted in a miraculous display of God's power (Acts 12:6–19). Prayer is to be the priority of Christ's church, because it is the means God has given for us to receive from His hand.

Life on the Altar for the Advance of the Gospel

When Paul appealed to the Romans for unity in the gospel, I'm confident he reflected upon his experiences from earlier years in Antioch. The memory of that beloved congregation, who laid their hands on him and sent him out, would be a comfort through many hard seasons of ministry. As Paul looked to new horizons for the gospel, he needed new partners who were committed to the truth and supportive in the same ways he experienced with the church in Antioch. Life on the Altar leads us to this kind of commitment.

Early in our missions development at FBCG, we began using the term "export" to describe our missions sending. We believed that by sending out teams we are "exporting" our local ministry. Because of that, we feel a heightened sense of commitment to the spiritual health of our church life. We are by no means perfect, and I am certainly not saying that a church needs to have everything in order before they begin obeying Acts 1:8. We are most definitely "in-process," and we need God's ongoing sanctifying work in our lives. My point is that we wanted to export a healthy ministry—Christ-exalting, kingdom-seeking, Bible-centered, church-planting, missions-mobilizing, and family-building. This is the missions ministry we long to export to the nations.

Our life in Christ is to be lived out in a local church where we commit together to the commission of our Savior. Our involvement in the local church family is a key partnership with others, seeking to accomplish what we could never do alone. Life on the Altar is to be lived together, and as we walk in the grace of God may we be confident that this is God's way of advancing His good news.

Altar Moments

1. How does the Antioch church's ministry challenge you with your church involvement? Your view of other members in the body? Your involvement in advancing the gospel through missions?

2. In this chapter, we identified how Barnabas, when he entered the gathering of the church, "saw the grace of God" (Acts 11:23). Do you have eyes to see God's grace on display in your life? In your church? How would that transform a critical, cynical spirit to one of gratitude?

3. With such a strong emphasis on prayer in the book of Acts, how engaged are you in prayer? Do you spend time in personal prayer daily for the success of your church's ministry?

Are you committed to the prayer gatherings of your church? Spend some time reading the prayer meetings recorded in Acts 1:12–2:4, 42–43; 4:23–31; 12:6–19; 13:1–3. What do you learn about the gathering of the church and the call to pray?

Prayer:

> "Lord Jesus, it's only because you were obedient to death—even death upon the cross—that we can offer back an obedience of grateful faith. Live and love, in us and through us…. Be magnified in our hearts, revealed in our cities, and revered among the nations of the world. We pray with great anticipation, in your most worthy name. Amen."[6]

---

6   Smith, *Everyday Prayers,* location 244, Kindle edition.

Before the
Throne of God Above

"And I heard a loud voice from the throne saying,
'Behold, the dwelling place of God is with man.
He will dwell with them, and they will be his
people, and God himself will be with them as
their God. He will wipe away every tear from
their eyes, and death shall be no more, neither
shall there be mourning, nor crying, nor pain
anymore, for the former things have passed
away." Revelation 21:3–5

ALTAR LIFE HAS A destiny beyond this world which takes
us to the throne of God above. The apostle Peter once
reminded Jesus, "We have left everything and followed you"
(Mark 10:28). Jesus responded by saying, "No one who has left
house or brothers or sisters or mother or father or children or
lands, for my sake and for the gospel, who will not receive a hun-
dredfold now in this time, houses and brothers and sisters and

mothers and children and lands, with persecutions, and in the age to come eternal life" (Mark 10:28–30). The New Testament never leads us to think that following Christ will somehow be dissatisfying. Yes, there will be disappointments and grief in this road marked by suffering, but we can be assured that this present groaning doesn't even compare to "the glory that is to be revealed to us" (Rom. 8:18).

Prior to His arrest and crucifixion, Jesus spoke to the disciples about His departure and imparted these words of future hope to them: "In my Father's house are many rooms. If it were not so, would I have told you that I go to prepare a place for you? And if I go and prepare a place for you, I will come again and will take you to myself, that where I am you may be also." (John 14:2–3).

Christ promised that the life He gives will be fuller and greater than anything this world can offer, with the best yet to come. From the beginning, redemption's plan was that God would gather a people for His glory, and the redeemed would live with Him forever and ever (Matt. 24:31; Eph. 1:3–14; Rev. 7:9–17). This is how the Bible ends in Revelation 21–22.

This promised future for those in Christ motivates us to live for that day when our faith shall be sight. The words of martyred missionary Jim Elliot bear repeating: "He is no fool who gives up what he cannot keep to gain that which he cannot lose."[1] Life on the Altar is a life motivated by an eternal perspective.

---

1 Elizabeth Elliot ed., *The Journals of Jim Elliot: Missionary, Martyr, Man of God* (Grand Rapids: Revell, 1978), 174, Kindle edition.

Paul presents this eternal mindset in the closing chapters of Romans. In Chapter 14, he wrote this word of comfort, "For none of us lives to himself, and none of us dies to himself. For if we live, we live to the Lord, and if we die, we die to the Lord. So then, whether we live or whether we die, we are the Lord's" (vv. 7–8). Paul followed this hopeful and clarifying word by saying, "We will all stand before the judgment seat of God; for it is written, 'As I live, says the Lord, every knee shall bow to me, and every tongue shall confess to God.' So then each of us will give an account of himself to God" (Rom. 14:10–12).

The Altar Life flowing from Romans 12 is one that anticipates eternal realities. Through the gospel, we have hope in this life and in the one to come. Through Christ, those who believe in Him have an Advocate who represents us before the judgment seat of God (1 John 2:1–2). Therefore, we live with hope in the certainties of God's promises. Paul expressed that confidence in Romans 15: "May the God of hope fill you with all joy and peace in believing, so that by the power of the Holy Spirit you may abound in hope" (v. 13). In Christ, our future is more than appearing before the judgment seat of God. God will bring forth a new heaven and new earth for His redeemed (Rev. 21).

Do you ever think about this eternal destiny? I'm not interested in supposed momentary journeys to heaven. I'm calling for the recovery of a biblically informed understanding of what we should anticipate before the throne of God above. It is life-changing to think about the picture God's Word gives to describe the future home of the believer. Why do we minimize the hope of heaven? Is it trivial to us? Maybe it is because heaven is trivialized constantly.

The Trivialization of Heaven

Some years ago, I prepared a series of messages on heaven. My research took me on a confusing journey. I learned that Bryan Adams had a song entitled "Heaven" which described heavenly bliss as having your girlfriend in your arms. Adams emotes in this rock anthem that love found in his girlfriend's heart is heaven indeed.

As I continued reading, I discovered a conflicting survey of beliefs about heaven from the various world religions. I spent some time on the ABC News website where Barbara Walters attempted to answer questions like, "Where is heaven?" and "How do you get there?" If you want clarity on heaven, don't bother going to Barbara Walters for any insight. Trust me!

Moving on with my search, I discovered there was a nightclub in Seattle called "Heaven," and there was a restaurant named "Burger Heaven." And of course, Disney has an animated film assuring us that *All Dogs Go to Heaven*. There also exists a manifest scorn for anyone insisting on an exclusive claim of who can enter heaven.

In many respects, our culture has been inoculated with a Jesus message, or worse, a "fairness doctrine" that falls short of the radical call of Christ. The popular path to heaven ignores the command of Christ who said, "Enter by the narrow gate.... for the gate is small, and the way is narrow that leads to life, and few are those who find it" (Matt. 7:13–14). In such a climate, heaven has become an entitlement—"heaven is for everyone"—and where everyone goes, except the really bad people of the world.

The words of the apostle John are clear about those who make it to heaven: "But nothing unclean will ever enter it, nor anyone who does what is detestable or false, but only those who are written in the Lamb's book of life" (Rev. 21:27). This book of life mentioned in Revelation 13:8, 17:8 and 20:12, 15 is a divine record of the names of all those whom God has chosen to save and who possess eternal life through faith in Jesus Christ.

Faithfulness to the gospel demands we embrace that there is a perishing for the unbelieving world. Jesus spoke of these eternal realities throughout His ministry. In Matthew 25, He uses the word "eternal" to describe both punishment and life (v. 46). Perhaps the most familiar verse in the Bible, John 3:16 contains a strong statement on the danger of perishing. Jesus' life and ministry was a saving mission centered on redeeming that which was lost (Luke 19:10). One of the most sobering passages in the Bible is Revelation 20 which describes the final judgment of the unredeemed. It is impossible to tone down or explain away verse 15: "And if anyone's name was not found written in the book of life, he was thrown into the lake of fire."

The teaching of an eternal punishment in hell is clearly presented in the Scripture. Randy Alcorn writes, "If we understood Hell even the slightest bit, none of us would ever say, 'Go to Hell.' It's far too easy to go to Hell. It requires no change of course, no navigational adjustments. We were born with our autopilot set toward Hell. It is nothing to take lightly—Hell is the single greatest tragedy in the universe."[2]

Viewing heaven as an entitlement with no fear of judgment is a serious deception. Along with the lame and flippant usages of "heaven" that permeate the church, as well as in popular culture, have impacted the way believers think about their eternal home. Our expectations and understanding of this glorious destiny have been dampened.

I understand how the world would misunderstand the hope of heaven, but what about God's people? When the subject of heaven does come up, often the conversation among believers tends to be, well, uninviting. Like an air conditioner out of Freon in the summer heat, it's just not refreshing.

In this closing chapter, I hope to challenge the colorless anticipations held by many with a biblical picture of the believer's destiny. Why do Christians talk so little about heaven when everything precious to the believer is there?

Everything Precious to the Believer

A survey of the New Testament reveals that everything of lasting value awaits us in heaven. Jesus warned about laying up treasures on earth. We know too well the uncertainties of earthly assets which are susceptible to theft and ruination. In short, they don't last. Jesus' teaching urges the following wisdom: "Lay up for yourselves treasures in heaven where neither moth nor rust destroys and where thieves do not break in and steal" (Matt. 6:19–20).

---

2   Randy Alcorn, *Heaven* (Carol Stream: Tyndale House Publishers, 2004), 27.

To be born again by the Holy Spirit (John 3:3) is to become a citizen of heaven (Phil. 3:20). Like Abraham, the believer in Christ is looking "forward to the city that has foundations, whose designer and builder is God" (Heb. 11:10).

Is this the way you live? Do you live with a vision of your eternal home in Christ? Some may be worried that to be too heavenly minded will render us useless in this world. I don't think we are endangered of that ever happening. One of the struggles believers face is that we are so consumed by horizontal living that we forget that our most precious treasures are in heaven.

When Jesus taught about His second coming, He said, "Now when these things begin to take place, straighten up and raise your heads, because your redemption is drawing near" (Luke 21:28). We need reminders to awaken us to realize that this world is not our home and that our Savior is returning … soon. Think with me for a moment of the precious treasures that await the believer when our earthly sojourn is complete.

Our Father Is in Heaven

Jesus began His model prayer with these words, "Our Father in heaven, hallowed be your name" (Matt. 6:9). Instructing His disciples on how to pray, He began with an acknowledgement that there is a God, who is a Father, and His dwelling place is heaven. Before this Father God, we live and move and exist, and one day we will see Him as He is (1 John 3:2). Such hope has a purifying power upon our lives. God is the ultimate treasure any creature could have.

I am reminded of God's calling of Abram (Abraham), but especially as the word of the Lord came to him in Genesis 15: "Fear not, Abram, I am your shield; your reward shall be very great" (v. 1). The reward to Abram, by virtue of God's covenantal promises, was His protection, provision, and presence. God said in effect, "Abram, I am your reward!" And the same is true for every believer in Jesus Christ.

Jonathan Edwards contributed greatly to the theology of the church, especially with his thoughts on God and eternity. Some 275 years ago, he preached a sermon from Matthew 5:8: "Blessed are the pure in heart, for they shall see God." Edwards said, "The fountain that supplies [the] joy and delight, which the soul has in seeing God ... is infinite.... How blessed therefore are they that do see God, who are come to this exhaustless fountain!... After they have had the pleasure of beholding the face of God millions of ages, it will not grow a dull story; the relish of this delight will be as exquisite as ever."[3] Edwards makes the point that heaven will in no way be boring because it will be an ever expanding, ever unfolding discovery of the person of God.

In the book of Revelation, the apostle John exhausts human language to communicate the glories of heaven. Read how he describes God as the center of it all: "And I saw no temple in the city, for its temple is the Lord God the Almighty and the Lamb. And the city has no need of sun or moon to shine on it, for the glory of God gives it light, and its lamp is the Lamb" (Rev.

---

3   Jonathan Edwards, *The Works of Jonathan Edwards Vol. 2* (Peabody, MA: Hendrickson Publishers, 1998), 909.

21:22–23). The glory of God illumines and blesses our eternal home without rival.

Our Savior Is in Heaven

Secondly, our Lord and Savior is in heaven. After His ascension, Christ was seated at the right hand of the throne of God (Heb. 1:3). This signified that His redeeming work had been completed to perfection, and He was given a place of prominence by God the Father. Again, in the book of Revelation, we read of the breathtaking splendor of the Lamb who was slain and is worthy to receive the praises of heaven's choir. The choir sings a new song of God's redeeming work through Christ:

> **Worthy are you to take the scroll and to open its seals,**
> **for you were slain, and by your blood you ransomed**
> **people for God from every tribe and language**
> **and people and nation, and you have made them a**
> **kingdom and priests to our God, and they shall reign**
> **on the earth. (Rev. 5:9–10)**

This seems to me one of the strongest arguments for the deity of Christ. If Christ were not God, heaven would be in discord, but it is not. Our triune God reigns in perfect unity in the counsel known from eternity past.

Charitie Bancroft captured this scene in her beloved hymn:

> Behold him there, the risen Lamb,
> My perfect, spotless righteousness;
> The great unchangeable "I AM,"
> The King of glory and of grace.
> At one with him, I cannot die;
> My soul is purchased by his blood.

My life is hid with Christ on high,
With Christ, my Savior and my God,
With Christ, my Savior and my God.[4]

For the believer, heaven should be cherished because our Savior is there, and He will gather the redeemed who will experience life as it was meant to be.

Fellow Believers in Christ Will Be There

Death keeps sloppy appointments and nowhere has that been more evident than in the COVID-19 pandemic. The years 2020–21 have been marked by abounding sorrows as this strange virus has ravaged beloved friends and relatives. We lost a dear brother in our church in 2020. For weeks, we agonized with his wife, Rosemary, as Steve declined under the cadence of a ventilator. When our prayers for Steve's healing were not answered in the way we hoped, we grieved deeply.

Because of COVID-19 concerns and a hurricane heading our way from the Gulf of Mexico, Steve's funeral was a graveside service. As we gathered at the cemetery and the casket of this beloved brother was brought to the freshly dug grave, spontaneous singing came from Rosemary and the family. The entire gathering quickly joined them as we sang: "He will hold me fast. He will hold me fast, For my Saviour loves me so, He will hold me fast."[5]

There was a baptism of the Lord's comfort at Steve's graveside that day. We gathered as Christians have through the centuries to remember the promises of God to those who die in the Lord.

4 Charitie Lees Bancroft, "Before the Throne of God Above," public domain.
5 Ada R. Habershon, *"He Will Hold Me Fast,"* public domain.

We rejoiced that Steve was not in that casket and remembered Paul's words to the Thessalonians, that in our grief we would "not grieve as others who have no hope. For since we believe that Jesus died and rose again, even so, through Jesus, God will bring with him those who have fallen asleep" (1 Thess. 4:13b–14).

Nearly a year after Steve's funeral, Rosemary texted me with this message, "He left our home by ambulance a year ago tomorrow. That day stands out in my mind as the last day we spoke face-to-face. God's timing is always perfect." A message typed with a broken heart, but not without hope in a future reunion around the throne of God, and a reminder that even at the graveside, resurrection is our song.

Our hope of being reunited in the presence of God was not an idea manufactured by some religious committee who thought such a narrative would be a good end to it all. Our belief is found throughout the Scripture with one promise after another. There is an assurance for God's people that gives peace in the most painful experiences in life, including the death of a loved one.

Martin Luther used to spend time teaching his children on Sunday afternoons. He taught them sound doctrine from a catechism he wrote. Luther had a 13-year-old daughter named Magdalena who was dying. Luther prayed as her condition deteriorated, "I love her very much. But if it is your will to take her, dear God, I will be glad to know that she is with you." And then Luther spoke to his daughter as her consciousness waned, "Magdalena, my little daughter, you would be glad to stay here with me, your father? Are you also glad to go to your Father in heaven?" Magdalena replied, "Yes, dear Father, as God wills."[6] And she fell asleep in Jesus.

Believers in Christ are destined for heaven through the trailblazing work of our Redeemer. The apostle Paul spoke for believers living in this veil of tears when he wrote that we "would rather be away from the body and at home with the Lord" (2 Cor. 5:8). When a believer dies, their spirit goes to be with Christ, awaiting the resurrection day when we receive a resurrection body in which we will live forever in the presence of God and among His redeemed (1 Cor. 15:50–57; 1 Thess. 4:13–18).

Joni Eareckson Tada has inspired many people since a diving accident in her youth rendered her a quadriplegic. Her joy over decades of ministry has inspired many to put their hope in Christ. She wrote in one of her books, "The first thing I plan to do on resurrected legs is to drop on grateful, glorified knees. I will quietly kneel at the feet of Jesus."[7] What a glorious hope!

Biblical truth informs our view of eternity. Tada is not throwing pennies in a wishing well when she speaks about her future resurrection body. Neither is she grasping at straws when she speaks of bowing at the feet of Jesus. Her hope is guided by the truth of Scripture, and this is a solid rock indeed. From the Word of God, we learn that our Father is in heaven, our Savior is in heaven, and our loved ones in Christ are destined for heaven. We could also include in this robust hope that: our citizenship as believers is in heaven (Phil. 3:20); our names are written in

---

6   *365 Days of Luther Quotes* (Milwaukee, WI: Northwestern Publishing House, 2016), 10.

7   Joni Eareckson Tada, *Heaven: Your Real Home ... From a Higher Perspective* (Grand Rapids: Zondervan, 2018), 70.

heaven (Luke 10:20); our reward is in heaven (Matt. 5:12); our inheritance is in heaven (1 Pet. 1:3–4), and our treasure is in heaven (Matt. 6:19–21).

Truly, everything precious to the believer is in heaven and this should provide strong motivation to keep seeking the things above where Christ is, seated at the right hand of God (Col. 3:1). We are to treasure this hope in our hearts and live for that day when we will appear before Him.

Presenting Ourselves to Him Forever and Ever

Life on the Altar is a prelude for eternity. Heaven will be an everlasting presentation of ourselves to God. Is that appealing to you? What does this mean and how should we envision such an eternal existence?

I mentioned that Randy Alcorn's work, *Heaven*, is a masterful guide to help believers think about the prospects of heaven. I commend it to you as a book worth every minute you give to it. In this work, Alcorn remained tethered to the biblical text, and yet explores questions and ideas that stretch our imagination and fuel our longings for what God has for His people. He offers these refreshing thoughts:

> The most ordinary moment on the New Earth will be greater than the most perfect moments in this life—those experiences you wanted to bottle or hang on to but couldn't. It can get better, far better, than this—*and it will*. Life on the New Earth will be like sitting in front of the fire with family and friends, basking in the warmth, laughing uproariously,

dreaming of the adventures to come—and then going out and living those adventures together. With no fear that life will ever end or that tragedy will descend like a dark cloud. With no fear that dreams will be shattered, or relationships broken.[8]

These are not hard thoughts to grasp in reading John's account in Revelation 21. The only life we have known has been the fallout from paradise lost in the garden of Eden. Is it so difficult to see Alcorn's words as reasonable when we read John's description, specifically, "He who was seated on the throne said, 'I am making everything new!' Then He said, 'Write this down, for these words are trustworthy and true'"? (Rev. 21:5). When John described the New Heaven and New Earth, the newness he referred to is not chronological, but qualitative. John was describing a place and a condition that is better than anything we could ever have envisioned and wondrously absent are all the things that make life in this world so painful. Think of the day when Christ ministers to His redeemed and "wipes away every tear from their eyes, and death shall be no more, neither shall there be mourning, nor crying, nor pain anymore, for the former things have passed away" (Rev. 21:4). No doubt this comfort of the Lord will be received with a collective expression of worship: "Worthy is the Lamb!" (Rev. 5:12).

James Hamilton gives help in understanding what it means for the Lord our God the Almighty to reign without rival: "This means the end of incompetent, unworthy, unqualified government. No more will God's world be troubled by those who

---

8 Alcorn, *Heaven,* 472.

cannot rule it. No more will God's world be troubled by those who rebel against his authority, reject his claim on them, refuse to be guided by his wisdom, and trouble those who honor the world's rightful Lord....When God begins to reign, the world will finally be ruled as it should be."[9]

The details of heaven will remain a mystery until our faith becomes sight, but the descriptions offered in God's Word are not shrouded. They are given to encourage believers to anticipate with excitement all that God has prepared for those who love Him. These closing scenes of the Bible describe a reality we have never known on this groaning planet as the Lord God makes all things right.

The aim of this book has been to encourage us to pursue Life on the Altar as preparation for what we will do in heaven with eternal satisfaction. I would like to conclude with a foretaste of things to come when we experience perfect worship, perfect rest, perfect work, and perfect adventure.

Perfect Worship

For some, the image of worship in heaven is their pastor, or some preacher, endlessly pontificating with interspersed music, "and so shall it ever be, forever and ever, Amen." That is certainly not a thought that is going to energize a thrill for heaven, but neither is it the picture of worship given in Revelation. In the text that inspired Handel's "Hallelujah" Chorus, John describes the centerpiece of heaven's worship in Revelation 19:

---

9   James M. Hamilton, *Revelation: The Spirit Speaks to the Churches* (Wheaton: Crossway Books, 2012), 350.

> **After this I heard what seemed to be the loud voice of a great multitude in heaven, crying out, "Hallelujah! Salvation and glory and power belong to our God, And from the throne came a voice saying, 'Praise our God, all you his servants, you who fear him, small and great."** (vv. 1–2, 5)

The presence of God calls for songs of loudest praise. In Revelation 21:3–4, we read, "No longer will there be anything accursed, but the throne of God and of the Lamb will be in it, and his servants will worship him. They will see his face, and his name will be on their foreheads."

Unlike awkward worship transitions and compartmentalized living that distract us from true worship, heaven's scene describes worship without hindrance and sin's disruption. We have never known a worship service that hasn't been impacted by our sin. However, every believer in some measure has experienced the nearness of God and the thrill of His presence in a time of worship. These experiences are deposits, foretastes, of greater things to come when our attention will be upon the One who has redeemed us and the endless blessings He has in store.

Perfect Rest

One of the beautiful applications of Christ's life, death, and resurrection is that He has become the sabbath rest of the believer (Heb. 4:1–11). In salvation, we rest in His finished work on our behalf. Believers press on in this fallen world to the honor of our King, and we labor in love and seek to glorify Christ with our lives. In heaven, we will experience perfect rest. Earlier in Revelation, John "heard a voice from heaven saying, 'Write this:

Blessed are the dead who die in the Lord from now on.' 'Blessed indeed,' says the Spirit, 'that they may rest from their labors, for their deeds follow them!'" (Rev. 14:13). All burdens and stresses that bear down upon us will be lifted as we come to the end of our sojourning. Our struggles with the world, our own flesh, and the evil one will be over.

Charles Spurgeon spoke of heaven as coming "home from exile, to come to land out of the raging storm, to come to rest after long labour, to come to the goal of my desires and the summit of my wishes."[10] Spurgeon died about a decade before his wife Susannah. Ray Rhodes, Jr. captured the hope the Spurgeons shared in his tender book entitled, *Susie*. As a grieving widow, Susie shared the hope of future reunion with her husband of thirty-six years: "It is my confident belief that I shall see and know my beloved again in glory, and that there, our earthly love, purified and sanctified, shall continue and maybe, increase in the perpetual light of the presence of our King and Saviour."[11]

Heaven's rest will be the ultimate fulfillment of Jesus' promise in salvation. Matthew 11 contains Jesus' call to sinners then and now: "Come to me, all who labor and are heavy laden, and I will give you rest" (v. 28). In Him, we will experience an eternal sabbath's rest, saved to sin no more and possessing every spiritual blessing that God has prepared for His people.

---

10 Charles H. Spurgeon, *Morning and Evening: Daily Readings* (London: Passmore & Alabaster, 1896), Morning, April 25th, Logos Bible Software.

11 *The Sword and the Trowel: A Record of Combat with Sin & Labour for the Lord* (London: Passmore and Alabaster, 1865–1904), 9, quoted in Ray Rhodes, Jr., *Susie: The Life and Legacy of Susannah Spurgeon* (Chicago: Moody Publishers, 2018), 182, Kindle edition.

Perfect Work

One might think that with perfect worship and rest that there would be no room for work, but such is not the case. When God placed Adam in the garden of Eden, one of the first things He did was give Adam a job. Heaven will be marked by work delivered from sin's curse. The passion, drive, and exertion many feel regarding their work will be redeemed for God's glory and our satisfaction. Endless opportunities will abound for us to build and create under the new order.

Perfect Adventure

With resurrection bodies, we will abide forever in a new creation and enjoy God's universe. Countless adventures await. Alcorn captures this better than anyone I've read:

> Not only will death not separate us from Christ—
> it will actually usher us into his presence. Then, at
> the final resurrection, Christ will demonstrate his
> omnipotence by turning death on its head, making
> forever alive what appeared forever buried. If you
> believe this, you won't cling desperately to this life.
> You'll stretch out your arms in anticipation of the
> greater life to come. If my descendants, perhaps
> my grandchildren or great-grandchildren, should
> read these words after I've died, know this: I'm
> looking forward to greeting you when you arrive
> in the intermediate Heaven (unless Christ returns
> in the meantime and we meet at the resurrection).
> I'll have some favorite places picked out for you,
> and we'll go there together. But we won't stay there

long. Ultimately we'll travel together to our true home, the New Earth. We'll settle and explore it side by side, as pioneers. What a world it will be. I'm overwhelmed just thinking of it. What a great God we'll enjoy and serve forever. What a great time we'll have together there. I look forward to seeing every reader who knows Jesus, meeting most of you for the first time, and being reunited with those I've known here on the present Earth. I can't wait for the great adventures we'll have with Christ and each other. Don't let a day go by without anticipating the new world that Christ is preparing for us. God loves the Heaven bound, but he is proud of the Heaven minded: "They were longing for a better country—a heavenly one. Therefore God is not ashamed to be called their God, for he has prepared a city for them" (Hebrews 11:16, emphasis added).[12]

With the promise of such a glorious future, we long for the blessed hope in the last verses of the Bible: "'Surely I am coming soon.' Amen. Come, Lord Jesus! The grace of the Lord Jesus be with all. Amen" (Rev. 22:20–21). Until that day, let's meet at the altar where we find His mercy and the strength to live the life He has called us to live.

Altar Moments

1. Do you think heaven has been trivialized? How have your thoughts about heaven been challenged or expanded in this chapter?

---

12 Alcorn, *Heaven*, 468.

2. Read 1 Corinthians 15:50–58; 1 Thessalonians 4:13–18; Revelation 21–22. What details do these passages give regarding future hope?

3. How does Jesus' promised return impact your response to Christ now? Would you receive Christ by faith and join us in this sojourn that ends in His very presence?

Prayer:

"Gracious Father,

Because of Jesus, we, your redeemed people, will go out in joy and be led forth into peace, into shalom— the perfect order, society, environment, and world of the new heaven and new earth. You have spoken, you have promised, and so shall it be! Your Word will accomplish everything you decree and all your delights. With great hope we pray in Jesus' name. Amen."[13]

---

13 Smith, *Everyday Prayers,* location 421, Kindle edition.

Epilogue

"The life I now live in the flesh I live by faith in the Son of God, who loved me and gave himself for me." Galatians 2:20

In July 2021, I happened to be in Enfield, Connecticut, on a ministry assignment. My hotel was less than five miles from a stone marker along Highway 5 which marked the location of the meeting house of the First Church of Christ. At that location, on July 8, 1741, Jonathan Edwards preached to his congregation perhaps the most popular sermon in American history, "Sinners in the Hands of an Angry God." This sermon was a catalyst for the First Great Awakening which swept through North America and impacted other parts of the world with a ripple effect to this generation.

As I stood in front of that stone with fellow elder, Russ Copeland, we prayed for God to move in our generation, specifically for there to be an awakening to hear the gospel and for God's

Word to run rapidly to needy hearts (2 Thess. 3:1). The spiritual needs are overwhelming. Believers must put off religious gimmicks and church games!

The prophet Jeremiah preached to the false messages of his day: "They have healed the wound of my people lightly, saying, 'Peace, peace,' when there is no peace" (Jer. 8:11). We need a move of God upon the church, but that won't come through more strategies or superficial remedies. We need to humble ourselves before God and live in the obedience of faith before a world that chafes under His reign. We need to live Life on the Altar, presenting ourselves to God in humble obedience.

As I conclude writing this book, the summer of 2021 has come to an end. This time of year serves as a reminder to me of our need to be right with God. When each August comes, I am reminded of another statement found in Jeremiah: "The harvest is past, the summer is ended, and we are not saved" (Jer. 8:20). These words were spoken by the people in a moment of anguish. It was a proverb expressing that their God-given opportunity to repent was now over. It was a statement of despair and loss.

Throughout their history, Israel's greatest enemies were not the Egyptians, or the Philistines, or the Assyrians, or the Babylonians. Israel's greatest enemies were the false prophets who stood in the gates and told the people what they wanted to hear. However, Jeremiah was not cut from that cloth of duplicity. By contrast, Jeremiah's preaching was a 'downer' for the hard-hearted nation of Judah. When Jeremiah confronted the sins of his people, he was persecuted. When he called the nation to repent, he was brought into the crosshair of their distain and abuse.

Jeremiah's singular message to repent and return to the Lord was grating on the nerves of many. I mean, really, how many times do you need to hear about your sins? How many times do you need to hear that you must repent and turn to the Lord? But faithful prophets don't custom craft their messages to please the people.

In Jeremiah's case, he preached for forty years with little response. Based on the numbers, he would never have been invited to be a speaker at an evangelism conference, and yet his fifty-two-chapter prophecy is encased in the canon of Scripture as a timeless example of pastoral perseverance.

He was a weeping prophet with a voice box committed to Yahweh and a heart to see the healing of his nation. But that healing would not come. Jeremiah would witness the Babylonian captivity in all its horror. Reading Lamentations records Israel's defeat as nothing short of brutal.

And yet, even in the agony of sin's consequences, Jeremiah would declare,

The steadfast love of the Lord never ceases; his mercies never come to an end; they are new every morning; great is your faithfulness. "The Lord is my portion," says my soul, "therefore I will hope in him." (Lam. 3:22–24)

This hope would find its fulfillment in the coming of Jesus Christ and is alive and powerful even to this moment. Jesus would begin his earthly ministry with the same message Jeremiah preached: "The time is fulfilled and the kingdom of God is at hand; repent and believe in the gospel" (Mark 1:15).

There is an urgency in the Scripture that calls us to put aside the mind-numbing distractions that fill our lives, and to be still and know that He is God (Psa. 46:10). We are admonished to examine ourselves spiritually to see if we are in Christ (2 Cor. 13:5). We are told not to boast about tomorrow because we do not know what a day will bring forth (Prov. 27:1). Things will not always be as they are. Today is a day of grace and refuge for the weary, and sin's relief is found in the person of Jesus Christ. However, there will be a time when the opportunity is gone and many will say to their great loss, "The harvest is past, the summer is ended, and we are not saved." Now is the acceptable time. Today is the day of salvation.

My hope for us in this journey has been to hear the call of God to present ourselves to Him as living sacrifices. This is the rightful response to Jesus' saving work. This relationship with God through faith in Christ is not to be lived in isolation: for Altar Life naturally leads to life in a local church. With all its flaws and shortcomings, the local church is the incubator God designed for our growth, nurture, and service. Through a local body, we join others in making Christ known to future generations as well as to the nations. After all, this was Christ's final word to His followers. May we also press forward in joy and in song, singing,

> Since Grace is the source of the life that is mine—
> And faith is a gift from on high—
> I'll boast in my Savior, all merit decline,
> And glorify God 'til I die.[1]

---

1   James Montgomery Boice, *Hymns for a Modern Reformation* (Philadelphia: Tenth Presbyterian Church, 2000), 25.